ADVAITA
AND
THE BUDDHA

RAMESH S. BALSEKAR

Books by Ramesh S. Balsekar

- Pursue 'Happiness' And Get Enlightened (2008)
- Celebrate the Wit & Wisdom: Relax and Enjoy (2008)
- Pointers From Ramana Maharshi (2008)
- Koun Parvah Karto?! (Marathi 2008)
- Does The Human Being Have Free Will? (2007)
- Enlightened Living (2007)
- A Buddha's Babble (2006)
- A Personal Religion of Your Own (2006)
- The Essence of The Ashtavakra Gita (2006)
- The Relationship Between 'I' And 'Me' (2006)
- A Homage To The Unique Teaching of Ramesh S. Balsekar (2006)
- Seeking Enlightenment – Why ? (2005)
- Nuggets of Wisdom (2005)
- The End of The Seeking (2005)
- Spiritual Search Step By Step (2004)
- Confusion No More (2003)
- Guru Pournima (2003)
- Upadesa Saram (2001)
- It So Happened That... (2000)
- Sin and Guilt: Monstrosity of Mind (2000)
- Meaningful Trivialities from the Source (2000)
- The Infamous Ego (1999)
- Who Cares?! (1999)
- The Essence of the Bhagavad Gita (1999)
- Your Head in the Tiger's Mouth (1997)
- Consciousness Writes (1996)
- Consciousness Strikes (1996)
- The Bhagavad Gita – A Selection (1995)
- Ripples (1994)
- Consciousness Speaks (1994)

ADVAITA
AND
THE BUDDHA

~

RAMESH S. BALSEKAR

EDITED BY
SUSAN WATERMAN

Previously published as
Advaita, the Buddha and the Unbroken Whole

First Reprint 2003
Second Reprint 2005
Third Reprint 2010

PUBLISHED BY

ZEN PUBLICATIONS
62, Juhu Supreme Shopping Centre,
Gulmohar Cross Road No. 9, JVPD Scheme,
Juhu, Mumbai 400 049. India.
Tel: +91 22 32408074
eMail: zenpublications@gmail.com
Website: www.zenpublications.com

CREDITS
Cover & Book Design by Red Sky Designs, Mumbai

ISBN 10   81-88071-57-9
ISBN 13   978-81-88071-57-9

₹ 300.00

PRINTED BY
Repro India Limited

This book is dedicated
to my son Ajit
(who died in 1990 at age 49)
who, having listened to most of the talks,
had no need for any reading
and
to all the seekers
for whom this reading is happening.

~

CONTENTS
~

Events happen, deeds are done, but there is no individual doer thereof.

THE BUDDHA
~

EVENT 2 REALITY – THE UNBROKEN WHOLE

EVENT 3: PART 1 THE HUMAN COMPUTER

ACKNOWLEDGEMENTS

~

I don't know how, nor do I think it is possible, to adequately or fully thank the Guru for all that is given – and all that is taken away – through Him. For the work on this book to happen through this body-mind organism is itself a gift from Shri Ramesh. It is yet another opportunity to swim in the ocean of the Teachings. The work, like reading this book, is another way of the Guru "taking the disciple back to the very Source of Manifestation itself." Thank you, dearest Ramesh, for shining light on the wholeness that life is. And thank you, Sharda, for your readings of the manuscript and for your daily welcoming of seekers into your home.

The initial inspiration for this book arose from three talks Ramesh had with an Australian Swami, a practising Buddhist monk. Our thanks to him and the others who happened to participate in those conversations. And thanks to Valeria Gallmann and her husband, Mario, through whom encouragement came for the transformation of those talks into book format. Valeria also shared her personal reflections from being present during the three conversations between Ramesh and Swamiji. In her writing, Valeria aptly expressed the gratitude felt by so many for Ramesh:

> *Thank you for being a Miracle, for so many, in the truest sense of the word – Miracle: Event due to supernatural agency, act of supernatural power, remarkable event, wonderful specimen of some quality. "Consciousness is all there is": no one other than Ramesh can lead one to that conclusion more rapidly or more convincingly. I thank Existence for having brought me to Your Feet.*

Kanwarjit Singh provided tapes of the satsangs used for this book. By his daily effort, many are able to carry home on audio CDs the words that happen through Ramesh. And thank you, Shirish Murthy, for insightful discussions on various topics in this book. Reliable and thoughtful editorial support, greatly appreciated, was always close at hand from Bianca Nixdorf and Chaitan Balsekar. And thanks to my husband, Clark, for his artistic contribution to the book cover, and for his patience throughout the editing process, particularly during the moments of futile fuss (sometimes noisy!) arising over a helpless, yet ever so necessary, programmed computer.

Lastly, ongoing gratitude arises for all the countless mysterious, seemingly miraculous, yet undeniable Divine occurrences in Unicity that enable such a book to happen.

~

Although it can be seen, the universe is nonetheless purely conceptual and has no actual substance or reality of its own.
All phenomena are nonexistent by nature.
Other than the primal Absolute subjectivity in which all exists, nothing in fact does exist!

– RAMESH BALSEKAR

≈

*One need only float with the magnificent current of
Totality in the ecstasy of oneness with the cosmic flow
of events. What else can the dreamer do with his dream
except passively witness it without judgement?*

– RAMESH BALSEKAR

∽

Note: The aphorisms of The Buddha placed throughout the
text were originally compiled by Paul Carus, *The Gospel of the
Buddha.* From: *The Sayings of Buddha,* Peter Pauper Press, Mt.
Vernon, N.Y., 1957 (no longer in operation).

EDITOR'S INTRODUCTION

≈

I was born into the world as the king of truth.
The subject on which I meditate is truth.
The practice to which I devote myself is truth.
The topic of my conversation is truth. My thoughts are
always in the truth. For lo! my self has become the truth.

Whosoever comprehends the truth will see
the Blessed One.

– THE BUDDHA

≈

In the words of the Buddha: *"Events happen, deeds are done, but there is no individual doer thereof."* The essence of Ramesh's teaching is the very same message: *"All actions are divine happenings through a uniquely programmed human object and not anyone's doing."* With the impact of these words during a talk, I'm sure there are as many different responses as there are people sitting there listening – depending, of course, on the programming of each, God's will and their destiny. The spectrum of responses – I might even dare say from agony to ecstasy – is often apparent from expressions on visitors' faces, from questions asked, or from comments following. Occasionally during a talk Ramesh may comment that pleasure or gratification arises when he sees one or several in the room being so receptive, when the teachings are going "straight to the heart". One person may walk away being struck by Ramesh as a brilliant orator or by the sheer flawless logic of it all. On the other hand, another may be bemoaning some feeling that he's been cheated because all the so-called Master did was to give out a bunch of concepts. Or yet another may stagger out, completely bewildered by the sense of having just fallen in love with this sage. Many walk away mystified but aware of the "something else" that goes on besides the talking, the "something that happens during the conversations, but only here," as one man named Michael recently put it. Ramesh is concerned only about conveying the teaching clearly – what else happens, knowing that it is God's will and the destiny of each particular body-mind organism, he's neither responsible nor concerned.

The apparent initial catalyst for this book was the happening of three conversations between Ramesh and an Australian Swami, a practising monk from a Buddhist tradition. Beyond those three talks, how did the [original] title for this book – *Advaita, the Buddha and the Unbroken Whole* – happen? Perhaps the key words are "Unbroken Whole" and "Advaita". First, "Advaita": Ramesh is a Master of Advaita, or Non-duality, the most important branch of Vedanta, the primary premise of which is *"All there is is Consciousness"*. Or, put another way, all phenomenal existence is an illusion. Hence, in Non-duality there is absence of a separate "me" as the actor, the doer. And what does "duality" mean? There are pairs of interconnected opposites, neither of which can exist without the other. Duality is the main mechanism by which the totality of the Manifestation operates, the very basis for life as we know it, life as it happens. However, Ramesh points out: "The ordinary person in every moment judges. The ego is not prepared to accept *what-is* in the moment." It is when the ego becomes involved in making an apparent choice between the interconnected opposites that duality becomes dualism, the whole becomes split.

Duality permeates every aspect of life, from so-called human personality to the tiniest unit known to quantum physics, which unit is in itself non-existent by its very nature! The ego gets involved in positive and negative, good and bad, beauty and ugliness, love and hate, male and female, etc., continually thinking there is someone to choose from something. This positioning becomes the basis for interhuman relationships, which must exist for life as we know it to happen. At the same time, pointing towards Totality, Ramesh emphasizes that "the human being cannot consider itself as an *individual* human being."

With great delight Ramesh speaks of the magnificence of life. He often reminds us of the role of seekers in all of it with the words of the well-known German mystic, Meister

Eckhart: *"All a seeker can do is wonder and marvel at the magnificence and diversity of God's creation."* Then Ramesh gently adds: "That's all a seeker can do, you see." In reference to life as it happens, drawing on the Hindu mythology, Ramesh recently said: *"The dance of Kali, the Divine Mother, is life as it happens, from moment to moment, bringing about all aspects of the interconnected opposites."* He elaborated with these words of Gary Zukav, a writer of science with an interest in Eastern philosophy:

> *"In Hindu mythology, Kali, the Divine Mother, is the symbol for the infinite diversity of experience. Kali represents the entire physical plane. She is the drama, tragedy, humor and sorrow of life. She is the brother, father, sister, mother, lover and friend. She is the fiend, monster, beast and brute. She is the sun and the ocean. She is the grass and the dew. She is our sense of accomplishment and our sense of doing worthwhile. Our thrill of discovery is a pendant on her bracelet. Our gratification is a spot of color on her cheek. Our sense of importance is the bell on her toe. This full and seductive, terrible and wonderful earth mother always has something to offer. Hindus know the impossibility of seducing her or conquering her and the futility of loving or hating her; so they do the only thing that they can do. They simply honor her."*

Perhaps the classic example of duality in Hindu philosophy is the concept of Shiva/Shakti. Ramesh described it this way: *"Shiva is the potential. Shiva is the Source. So Shiva in Its manifestation is Shakti or energy. Shiva does nothing. Shiva functions through Its mate, Shakti. Shiva, the Source, is undivided. When It manifests, It becomes two – Shiva-Shakti – and the entire manifestation is based on duality. So, without Shiva, Shakti cannot exist. And without Shakti, Shiva is Potential unmanifested."* Shiva is the Unbroken Whole.

Similarly, Advaita runs throughout the *Bhagavad Gita,* the classic dialogue between Lord Krishna and Arjuna in the Mahabharata. In Chapter VIII/20 it is said, *"Behind the manifest and the unmanifest (which concerns phenomenality) there is another Noumenal Awareness which is eternal and changeless – this is not dissolved in the general cosmic dissolution. This imperishable Unmanifest Awareness is said to be the highest state of being. Those who reach It do not return."*

From the perspective of science, in nature, at the level of molecules, pairs of interconnected opposites are essential for life to happen also. The whole simply cannot exist without the interconnected opposites. Take, for example, just two of the primary physiological or biochemical systems of the human body, and of all higher animals, necessary for life: first, the stuff of genes, the elegant molecular structure of the genetic material, DNA (deoxyribonucleic acid) and RNA (ribonucleic acid), where not only do two "strands" of the same type of molecule exist and function in tandem, but precisely paired molecules of matched polarity also must join together to bring about their necessary effect, which is the synthesis of yet another type of molecule. A protein is made, which subsequently may act in tandem with the molecule from which it was made, its template, or another molecule of its same kind, another protein, perhaps an enzyme, to bring about yet another necessary biochemical reaction. And, second, in the endocrine system, the complex system of hormones and their corresponding receptors, again stated very simply, the molecules must act in concert like two matching pieces of a jigsaw puzzle to elicit the most subtle and complex responses of the human body, both physical and psychological, to the environment. Though they are essentially "floating" in a liquid solution, the meetings of two molecules are neither random nor chosen – they must happen. In every living system, the examples go on and on of structurally and functionally paired molecular "opposites" requisite for life to happen.

Somewhere simultaneously between and beyond the level of measurable molecules and physical systems which appear to be entities unto themselves, like plant or animal tissues, organs and bodies, fall the observations which comprise the recently developed holographic model of the universe. By the use of very "pure" light, laser light, photographic images are generated which have revealed that every piece of nature contains the essence of the whole. Experiments have shown that if a film with a holographic picture of some intact object, say an apple, is cut into small pieces, each piece of film viewed again with laser light is seen to contain the whole object, a tiny apple! And, in somewhat similar experiments using special photographic plates sensitive to a highly refined type of light or energetic pattern, it has been demonstrated that if a hole is cut in a leaf from a plant and the leaf is then electrographically imaged, what appears is an image of the leaf with the hole, and within the hole is yet a second complete image of a tiny intact leaf! The implication of both types of experiments is that the universe exists as more than a summation of independent interacting parts, but rather as an uninterrupted whole. The fully integrated whole known by the mystic is tangibly brought into the reach of the ordinary man.

The "Unbroken Whole" becomes even more apparent at yet another level of resolution, in quantum physics. Physicists have shown that anywhere in the universe at any given moment two, shall we say invisible, particles "know" what the other is doing, evidenced by their measured movements. Given this relationship and the tentative evidence of an energy travelling even 300 times faster than the speed of light, is not the suggestion that the basis for all "existence" is totality, an Unbroken Whole, or "Consciousness is all there is"? Recently Ramesh commented: *"The implication of quantum mechanics is that the billions of objects in our universe – including human beings – appear to exist independently of one another, but that they are in fact parts of ONE all encompassing organic pattern. No parts of this one pattern are ever really separate from either the pattern itself, nor from one another."*

The concept of non-duality, or Totality, runs throughout all philosophies and can be seen as the basis for all religions: stated simply as four words from the Bible, "Thy Will Be Done". The alleged differences among religions, which have had tragic consequences throughout the history of mankind, appear as the result of interpretation, a masked marauder of the insidious sense of doership. Without this sense of doership, which is the core of the human ego and which is absent in the sage, what manifests is the Unbroken Whole. Ramesh repeatedly and emphatically states that for the sage the total awareness that is there all of the time is: *"No one does anything."* All actions are divine happenings though a particular body-mind organism just as they are supposed to happen at any and every given moment according to God's will.

Ramesh emphasizes that spiritual seeking is about and for life as we know it, not in some other time or place or body. Similarly, the Buddha explained:

The way of the Teacher requires every man to free himself from the illusion of the self, to cleanse his heart, to give up his thirst for pleasure, and lead a life of righteousness. And whatever men do, whether they remain in the world as artisans, merchants, and officers of the king, or retire from the world and devote themselves to a life of religious meditation, let them put their whole heart into their task; let them be diligent and energetic, and if they are like the lotus, which, although it grows in the water, yet remains untouched by the water, if they struggle in life without cherishing envy or hatred, if they live in the world not a life of self but a life of truth, then surely joy, peace and bliss will dwell in their minds.

Seeking happens and it is for here and now. Out of compassion, without any frills or hesitation, Ramesh frequently refers to how the sage lives his life in society, participating in life just as actively as an ordinary person, enjoying the pleasures of life and suffering the pains and hurts of life like any ordinary person, but without a load of pride or guilt or hatred or jealousy or envy. *"Put another way, in the words of the Buddha, the sage participates in the life that is sorrow ('Samsara is Dukkha') but enjoys the peace (Shanti) of Nirvana, at the same time. He thus proves the words of the Buddha: 'Samsara is Dukkha, Nirvana is Shanti, but they are not two'."*

So much joy bubbles up, just seeing the magnificence of life as it streams through Ramesh as he beckons everyone to flow along with life as it happens, with the Unicity. The magnificence that shines through the Guru I believe comes from the very living of life with complete and total humility, with the surrender that is innate, absolute, unremitting acceptance of the interconnected opposites which are life as it happens. Both the living of life and life as it happens are fully whole moment-to-moment. In this way, the Guru, by his very being, reflects the Unbroken Whole and points the way to all who are looking. Indeed, the very absence of separation is the wellspring of Love, the essence of the Unbroken Whole.

What follows is a personal account written by Valeria Gallmann, from Italy; it happened that she was present for the conversations which were the apparent catalyst for this book. Valeria shares her reflections on the unfolding of the talks between Ramesh – pure Advaita – and the Buddhist monk.

VALERIA WRITES

Ramesh's Teaching began for Mario, my husband, and me before we ever actually met him, not because we had read any of his books, but in the very way we came to him. That meeting in itself was the most peremptory example of what we later came to know as "His Concept". One day as we were driving along the highway, I was saying to Mario: "There are some people that you know will always be your friends, no matter what happens." In reply to his question: "Like whom?", I said: "Salila". Even before I had finished saying her name the phone rang and, surprising or not surprising, depending on your sense of the "not-ordinary", it was Salila calling from Bombay to say that she had been sitting for the last three days with an "extra-ordinary" Being, a true Sage, and that she had this urge to call us, that this thought was persistent, and now she was delivering the message, "You have to come, I know it is important." She described Ramesh as "The one man who can best put into words what cannot be said." (I find this to be a fitting description to this day!) Two days later we found ourselves in a plane on the way to India.

Until it happened that I met Ramesh, no Teacher, no book that crossed my path ever yielded the cherished "secret": I hadn't encountered that one concept, one word, one magic touch that would bring sudden clarity of the kind you cannot "lose" under any circumstances. Peace at all times as a possible state of being was a utopian dream until meeting Ramesh. He was able to convey a clear conceptual image of the bondage, of what the shackles really are, substantially, in life. "What do I really want to be liberated from?" Ego, yes, he is the recognized enemy, by all Schools. All Paths, from East and West, agree on Selflessness, but what is it? How do I recognize it? Can I separate "ego" and "me"? How? Those questions were mine. No one had ever pointed out clearly what the ego is, in terms I could not only understand but, more importantly, could not refute. From the very first day, I felt his concept "No 'One' does anything" was a radical guideline, something I could carry in my daily living as a constant reference point.

I had always felt the "responsibility" (to say the least!) of having this Soul, and this one life to "advance" it towards Liberation. Ramesh's welcome was to lift this burden, using the most stringent logic and concepts so consistently verifiable by past and present experience as to satisfy even the most analytical mind. He goes as far as saying: "Try it, put it to the test, this concept. Experience it with your ego. You have to be totally, utterly convinced with your whole being that no You ever existed at any time. Life just happens, Consciousness is all there is." "Do I really exist?", "Who am I?" For me, these questions ceased to be mere intellectual toys, ways of dissecting my personality, without resolution. "God's Will Be Done", words so often heard, so seldom heeded, take an unprecedented authority when spoken by Ramesh.

Last February, during one of our visits to Mumbai, a Buddhist monk came to Ramesh. For three days he sat in the talks and asked his burning questions. There was such an openness, a receptivity, such intensity in enquiry, plus the fore-knowledge of all the "theory", all the conceptual construction the intellect has fabricated to explain Truth, that the dialogue that took place was the most delightful I have ever witnessed. Looking back on the event and wanting to describe it, Socrates comes to mind, where Ramesh is Socrates, already beyond the reach of doubting mind, and the Swami is a "Philosopher", with all the necessary knowledge within but as yet not manifest in its integrated living form.

It was a wonder to witness the Teachings of the Buddha, no different in essence from the pure Advaita that Ramesh embodies, take shape before the Swami's consciousness. I felt that finally all the wisps of intuited Truth came before his eyes, and a clarity was reached that did not stem merely from belief but from direct apperception of what-is, now and always. I was particularly touched and impressed by Ramesh's genuine interest in what the Buddha's words were in regard to specific matters. With humility, he would respond to the Swami's query and then ask what the Enlightened One had said on the same topic. Consistently, the very same concept was revealed in different terms, different words, but identical "pointers". The essence was One.

One of the big issues was, of course, karma, understood as the individual Soul's progression towards Liberation through a succession of lives and its personal evolution, through "your" effort. Ramesh's flawless reasoning brings many, including myself, to a re-evaluation of this approach. Karma is wrought by the consequences of all actions, agreed! But whose actions? In the

Totality of Manifestation, how can one presume to judge anyone's deeds if, as all religions say, but so readily forget: "All is God's Creation." Hitler was as much part of God's Manifestation as was Gandhi, is Ramesh's uncompromising message. There is a "Pool of Consciousness" from which "individuals" are created by the Source, according to a Plan we can never know. The way Ramesh was able to expose this point was so convincing, so naked, that the Swami was apparently able to accept the only fundamental difference between his belief and what was being told by this Sage. There is nothing "personal" in karma and nothing you can do to change it. There was no opposition from the Swami, no pre-conceived idea came up to cloud the full perception, the impact of what Ramesh was saying.

The man's integral earnestness was revealed by his not using his "creed" to fend-off any "novel" interpretation. A genuine seeker was sitting there, absorbing the "conceptual Truth" from One who has the Ultimate Understanding. Ramesh's well-loved quote from the Buddha,"Events happen, deeds are done, but there is no individual doer thereof", found confirmation in the Swami's knowledge: he referenced it as in the Lankhavatara Sutra. Ramesh's great skill as a Teacher is to be able to pin-point the ego so accurately, so consistently, through its mutations, from all angles (however many you can come up with!). Eventually from a "formless" concept, ego is made recognizable as "involvement" – any kind of involvement, including the seeking.

Mario and I shared with others who were present the

feeling that the Swami had been "answered". He seemed to be awed by the Living Truth: he had devoted his life to "The Search" and here he could question it and receive the kind of answers that cut the head off of all questions. On the last morning, I perceived the Swami's utmost wonderment. He was leaning forward, keenly watching Ramesh in a very penetrating way, and his whole attitude seemed to be saying: "Here is the very State I have been searching for in the form of this man. All the scriptures are His own knowledge. He has no more doubts, so it is possible! This Being has attained 'Buddhahood', now alive and not confined to another age." There was relief and inspiration.

To witness a "full-time" seeker, one like the Swami, whose life has been devoted to Truth, moving towards an understanding of Reality, beyond words, to the very essence of what a human can perceive, not as a belief, but by having it demonstrated in practice, in both words and action, in presence, is a joyous event. Ramesh seems so ordinary, so simple, and yet as he teaches, his authority is felt; you just know that he is exactly what he says, No One. His Teaching is "down to the bones" and out of compassion he passes on only what is essential, what is needed to understand, no extra weight! God's Grace and destiny are sometimes easy to accept; on the other hand, sometimes the ego would like to claim its "importance" again and again as one is made to feel the lack of control, the impossibility of "running your life" as you wish it. Yet, life is full of surprises! One may end up wondering why the same conclusion had not been reached earlier – it becomes so obvious. If scrutinized with honesty, it cannot be refuted that everything boils down to circumstances and programming, which leaves "you" out of the picture.

So, to watch this monk, devoted to an ascetic existence, being told that even this was not his doing, his acquired merit to be carried from one life to the next, but simply his destiny, unfolding as part of the Manifestation, God's choice not his, was a revelation for me. He did not resent this concept, opposite to his familiar one, the Buddhist's "Intentional Right Living", according to which any individual is very much the single constructor of one's own Soul. Instead, I felt he took Ramesh's explanations as the unveiling of the most cryptic parts of the Scriptures of his tradition. The inspiration that only One who lives without a sense of personal doership can transmit, only He can give you the courage to try it. No books can do that.

"Yes! Yes! Yes!" was the exultant cry from within when Ramesh first delivered his concept, when this "Map to Wise Living" was handed to me. Nothing happens unless it is the will of God: the acceptance that a human object cannot do any different thing other than what it was programmed to bring about, like all the billions of other human objects, was, for me, a step towards Peace. Ramesh's view is not a passive, nihilistic attitude; on the contrary, it is a vibrant witnessing of an instrumental participation in life, this lila, as you enjoy playing your part, "Doing what you think you should do", keeping in mind, if you can, that it is not you doing anything! That is pure Buddhism and pure Advaita, pure Wisdom.

The moments of clarity that the Swami appeared to experience through Ramesh's guidance were uniquely exquisite for me. The conversation was one of those rare occasions when one could watch the Consciousness being fulfilled.

⁓

The "clarity" referred to by Valeria is indeed freedom from conceptual bondage, which is a basic theme of the talks that follow. Conceptual bondage is the sole factor that separates the ordinary man from the Unbroken Whole, that makes the ordinary man different from a sage.

⁓

Brahman

In the highest golden sheath is Brahman, stainless, whole. It is pure, the light of all light. This is what the knowers of the Self know. The sun does not shine there, nor the moon, nor the stars; there lightnings do not shine: where then could this fire be? The shining of the Self illumines the entire world. This that is deathless is indeed Brahman.

Mundaka Upanishad

∽

Emptiness

Where water, earth, heat and wind find no being, where no stars shine, where no sun can be seen, where no moon reflects light, where the darkness is not found. When the brahmin, the sage knows this place within himself, he is freed from both the form and the formless, from happiness and unhappiness.

The Udana

∽

Note

The unidentified aphorisms that introduce sections of the talks that follow are from Ramesh S. Balsekar.

Event 1: Part 1

~

You do not get on with life - life gets on with you and thousands and billions of other human objects.

Advaita And The Buddha

~

Consciousness Is All There Is

RAMESH Yes, Swamiji. What brings you here? What can I do for you?

SWAMIJI I am a Buddhist, so I am thinking of seeing life's problems with the idea that nothing is happening.

RAMESH Yes. So who told you nothing is happening? Buddhists told you nothing is happening?

SWAMIJI That's my understanding of Vedanta...

Ramesh ... No ...

Swamiji ... that everything is a play of, say, Consciousness.

Ramesh Yes, but it is a play; so when you watch the play – of course it's a play – who says there is nothing on the stage?

Swamiji So, there is something happening?

Ramesh Of course there is something happening, and that is life. What we call that happening is life. That which is happening, we call it life.

Swamiji So, what is the meaning of *maya?*

Ramesh *Maya* is what you see on the stage. What you see on the stage; what happens after the show is over?

Swamiji Everyone goes back to their normal...

Ramesh So, there is nothing on the stage. If you see a movie, you see the movie, you respond to it. If there is a tragic scene, tears may come; if there is a joke, you laugh. So you participate in the movie. But is the movie real? Isn't the movie an illusion – an illusion which appears on the screen? So the idea is that life as we see it is a movie which appears on the screen of Consciousness. The screen is always there, Consciousness is always there. Sometimes when this movie is happening, you watch it. When you are in deep sleep there is no movie. There is no life when you are in deep sleep. So that which you saw during the waking state, it disappears in your deep sleep.

Therefore it is not always there. That is, you can call it an illusion – *maya*.

SWAMIJI Is Consciousness something apart from its contents?

RAMESH Consciousness is the screen, the movie is something which appears on it. So Consciousness is always there. Consciousness is the only Truth, if the definition of Truth is something that is there all the time. It never is not. That is the Truth and that is Consciousness, that is Reality. So the only Reality is Consciousness, which is always there. Even in deep sleep...

SWAMIJI So, when you are saying that is the only Reality – (pointing) she is here, but she is not what I think she is. Is that it?

RAMESH No, she is not there when you are in deep sleep.

SWAMIJI But she is surely. You mean when I fall to sleep the whole world ceases to exist?

RAMESH Yes, the whole world ceases to exist.

SWAMIJI To me, but not objectively...

RAMESH Wait a minute. What you are saying is you may be asleep but the whole world is not. That is what you are saying. How do you know?

SWAMIJI Because when I wake up there it is again.

RAMESH That is your perception. They must be awake; I am in deep sleep – but you assume the others are awake. Supposing, Swamiji, the Consciousness or God makes it happen that during a particular two hours everybody is asleep, who is to say whether the world exists or not? If God makes it so happen any particular two hours everybody is asleep, who is to say there is a world outside which is seen by someone else? There is no one else.

SWAMIJI So are you saying it would cease to exist? Is there a difference between "it would cease to exist" or "it would cease to exist for all those who are asleep"?

RAMESH No. It would cease to exist for one reason, which, not only the Hindu mystic would say, but the physicist says now: an object exists only if it is observed. The physicist says this.

CONCEPTS – NOT TRUTH

SWAMIJI They might be wrong too, of course.

RAMESH So, everybody could be wrong. Then what are we talking about, Swamiji? What on earth are we talking about? If what anybody says could be wrong, and it could, I agree, then what are we talking about? Therefore, one of my basic concepts is that anything anybody has said so far, anything any sage has said, anything any scripture of any religion has said, is a concept. A concept is something which is liable to interpretation, and therefore will be acceptable to some and not acceptable to others. That is my definition of a concept. Based on that definition, what I am saying is what any sage has said at any time, what any scripture of any religion has said at any time is a concept, isn't it?

SWAMIJI Yes it is.

RAMESH Why do we have wars? Because the scriptures of one religion are not acceptable to another, the principles of one religion are not acceptable to another. So, is there any Truth at all, which according to this definition is not liable to interpretation and therefore cannot be denied by anyone? Is there any Truth at all, the Truth being something which cannot be interpreted and therefore will not be unacceptable to anyone? What do you think? What does the Buddha say? Is there any Truth at all according to this definition?

SWAMIJI Well, the Buddha has his concepts, too. But, for myself, I don't know. I don't think I could answer that. I could only say I suppose that when one actually *knows,* then there is nothing to argue about.

TRUTH: IMPERSONAL AWARENESS OF BEING

RAMESH The Truth according to this definition is the *Impersonal Awareness of Being,* I Am, I Exist. The *Impersonal Awareness of Being:* "I will be there whatever my name is." The *Impersonal Awareness of Being,* which no one can deny, is the only Truth, and the moment I talk about it, it becomes a concept. The *Impersonal Awareness of Being* is the only Truth, you see. The moment we think about it, it becomes a concept; the moment we talk about it, it becomes a concept.

VISITOR In deep sleep is it also there?

RAMESH Yes, I'll tell you why. When you wake up, do you not say: "I slept well" or "I didn't sleep well"? See, if there is no awareness at all, who is it saying she slept well or she didn't sleep well? So there is some kind of awareness. There is some kind of awareness, and the fact that it is not personal means that it is an *impersonal* awareness. The difference is that during the waking state the person is there. So, my basic concept is that the Reality is the *Impersonal Awareness of Being* which is covered by the screen of the individual personality.

VISITOR So this impersonal awareness, it's the same thing, it's still there, like when everybody goes to sleep, when there is nothing there?

RAMESH Yes, Impersonal Awareness is there because that is the only thing. I mean, to that extent that is also a concept. To accept that there is a Reality, a Source from which everything has come, that is the basic concept. There has to be a Source, One without a second, from which has emerged this Manifestation, and at the end of this emergence it goes back into the Source. Even that is a concept if we talk about it. The most apt simile for this emergence of the Manifestation is given in the *Bhagavatam:*

"As the spider weaves its thread out of its own
mouth, plays with it and then withdraws it again
into itself, so the eternal unchangeable Lord,
who is without form, without attributes, who is
absolute knowledge and absolute bliss, evolves the
whole universe out of Himself, plays with it for a
while, and again withdraws it into Himself."

So, if there is a Source which is there all the time,
that is the Consciousness, the Impersonal Awareness,
Consciousness-at-rest. Before the manifestation has come
about, is Consciousness-at-rest, which is not aware of itself.
Call it Potential Energy. But once the Potential Energy has
activized itself into this Manifestation, Consciousness-in-
movement is the Impersonal Awareness.

"LIFE" AS WE KNOW IT

RAMESH What is a human being? The answer would seem
to be a "living" object, as distinguished from a stone. We
would normally think of a human being as living and a
stone as not living, but as a matter of fact there is no way
we can either prove or disprove this! It could be that our
responses to events are as rigidly programmed as those
of a stone or a chemical, the only difference being that
we are programmed in a much more complex manner. It
could be that the human being does not have any more
freedom of action than a stone does, though of course the
human being deceives himself into thinking that he does!
In other words, it could be that an "inanimate" object
may be living as surely as a human being.

It would seem that the distinction between "animate" and "inanimate", between "organic" and "inorganic", is really nothing more than a conceptual one. Quantum mechanics seems not to support this concept. The human being is organic because he can make a decision by responding to processed information. The astounding fact is that according to the evidence of quantum mechanics, subatomic "particles" appear to be constantly making decisions! Indeed, such decisions seem to be based on information processed elsewhere.

∼

There is only one state. When corrupted and tainted by self-identification, it is known as an individual. When merely tinted by the sense of presence, of animated consciousness, it is the impersonal witnessing. When it remains in its pristine purity, untainted and untinted in primal repose, it is the Absolute.

— RAMESH BALSEKAR

∽

Event 1: Part 2

~

Paradoxical though it may seem: There is a path to walk on, there is walking being done, but there is no traveller. There are deeds being done, but there is no doer. There is a blowing of the air, but there is no wind that does the blowing. The thought of self is an error and all existences are as hollow as the plantain tree and as empty as twirling water bubbles.

Therefore as there is no self, there is no transmigration of a self; but there are deeds and the continued effects of deeds.

– The Buddha

~

The Human Being: One Species Of Object

Enlightenment Is An Event

Ramesh   There has to be a Source, ONE without the second, from which has emerged this Manifestation and at the end of this emergence it goes back into the Source. Even that is a concept if we talk about it.

SWAMIJI Why does that happen? And, if it happened once, should one become Enlightened, why couldn't it happen again?

RAMESH "Should one become Enlightened?" If you can explain that to me, then we can talk further. My concept about Enlightenment, Swamiji, is this: the happening of Enlightenment is an event in the functioning of Manifestation, or life as we know it. No *one* can become Enlightened. No 'one' can become Enlightened because who is this *one* we are talking about being Enlightened or not being Enlightened – who is the *one*? What do you say, who is this *one* who wants to be Enlightened?

SWAMIJI Well, from a Buddhist point of view, I would say it is just this bundle of consciousness and concepts and ideas and feelings and experiences.

RAMESH Yes. But basically my concept about the one who wants Enlightenment is: the human is one object, one species of object, which together with thousands of other species of objects constitute the totality of Manifestation. What is the Manifestation which has emerged from the Source? It is a collection of objects, from the planet to the individual body, it is an object. So, basically, what I am saying, Swamiji, is that every human being is fundamentally only an object, one species of object, which together with other thousands of species of objects on land, air and water constitute the totality of objects which is the Manifestation. So, how can an object be Enlightened?

GURU–DISCIPLE RELATIONSHIP

A true Guru is concerned not with changing the world or the behavior of the disciple but only with taking the disciple back to the very source of manifestation itself.

SWAMIJI OK, I've got to rephrase my question then. Why is the Guru-disciple relation important? Why are you teaching, why are these people coming here? There must be some will, some reason, it must be to bring about some change or restructuring, or...

RAMESH Yes, certainly. So, that restructuring of the perspective and attitude, the restructuring of the perspective and the attitude in that *object* is Self-realization or Enlightenment, brought about by the Source, who is bringing about the functioning of the Manifestation. What is life? The functioning of the Manifestation; and in the functioning of Manifestation which is life as we know it, Enlightenment is one event. So what does Enlightenment mean? What does it mean to you, Swamiji, if I may ask?

SWAMIJI Speaking again from the Buddhist perspective...

RAMESH Yes, of course.

SWAMIJI ...the Buddhist would say the realization is that there is no self.

RAMESH There is no self, meaning the individual?

SWAMIJI That which we identify with is not.

RAMESH That is the individual, isn't it, "me", "me". So Enlightenment is the total acceptance, that *total unconditional* acceptance without the slightest doubt, that the "me" as an individual entity with a sense of personal doership does not really exist. In other words, I don't live my life, life is being lived through this object. That is my definition of Enlightenment, which seems to agree with yours.

SWAMIJI Except maybe for one thing, if I may?

RAMESH Sure, sure.

SWAMIJI Here the Buddha would say something can be done to hasten or bring about that restructuring. My understanding of your teaching, or Vedanta, is that the Source will do that, that nothing you can do or the individual can do can hasten that or change that.

RAMESH Yes, why? Because basically, fundamentally, the one who you say would be able to do something about it is merely an object, merely *an object,* one species of object which together with thousands of other species constitute the totality of the Manifestation, which is a collection of objects.

SWAMIJI One must have painted oneself into a corner thereby. You are teaching; Vedantic teachers do talk about the importance of the Guru-disciple relationship.

RAMESH Certainly. Yes.

SWAMIJI So how does this fit in with that?

RAMESH So, as part of life, *as part of life*. In the words of the Buddha: "Events happen, deeds are done, but there is no individual doer thereof." I wasn't sure of the source. Someone offered to find it for me, a scholar, and she sent me an article; it was here, but it disappeared. Some other Buddhist scholar must have borrowed it and forgot to return it! But, from memory, which I don't myself trust, the name as I recollect is *Shri Lankhavatara Sutra*. Is there something like that? So, if you refer to it, maybe you will find it in that.

So, "events happen, deeds are done, but there is no individual doer thereof." The basic question, really, according to me is, if we are all objects, if there is no individual doer thereof, who is the doer? The Source, the Reality, Consciousness, God, Noumenon, whatever you call it, but once you call it something, give a label, the Limitless becomes limited. But nonetheless, because we have to talk, conceptually we have to limit the Limitless, otherwise we could just be in the Beingness – no problem!

SWAMIJI But, what you are saying is that one spiritual practice is, metaphorically, to put one's feet up, light up a cigarette and just wait or just be.

RAMESH If you can...

SWAMIJI What if you can't?

RAMESH If you can't, you can't! But what you are saying is: "I can. It's up to me, it's up to me to do what I want, it's up to me to do spiritual practices and attain, achieve Enlightenment."

SWAMIJI I see that as a problem, it's true. But I can't see any way around it. It seems that the alternative is to just light up a cigarette and go on with life.

RAMESH But "go on with life" – what I am saying is, you, Swamiji, do not get on with life: life gets on with you. *You* do not get on with life. Life gets on with you and thousands and billions of other human objects. That is why I keep saying: "I don't live my life, my life is being lived." And by whom? By the Source!

EVERY HUMAN BEING IS AN OBJECT

MARK How is the deepest possible understanding that there is no individual doer of any actions achieved?

RAMESH Achieved...? Your name is?

MARK Mark, from Australia.

RAMESH So, Mark, could you repeat your question, please?

MARK So, how is the deepest possible understanding that

there is no individual doer of any actions achieved?

Ramesh Achieved by whom, Mark?

Mark Achieved...

Ramesh By an object? Can an object achieve anything, Mark?

Mark Why do we limit to just that thing?

Ramesh So, my basic fundamental concept is, can an object achieve anything, can an object do anything? It can't, it can't. That's why the Buddha said there is no individual doer: "Events happen, deeds are done, but there is no individual doer thereof" – very specific. So, my interpretation of that is that every human being is an object, is a uniquely programmed object, a uniquely programmed computer, an object through which the Source brings about the deeds. Therefore there is no individual doer. I repeat, according to my basic concept, every human being is a uniquely programmed instrument, object, or computer, through which the Source or God or Consciousness, or whatever, brings about the deeds which the individual ego thinks is his action, his deed, and the Source uses every human computer exactly as the human being uses his own computer. How does a human being use his computer? He puts in an input and the programmed computer has no choice but to bring out an output strictly according to the programming. The computer has no choice. On the contrary, the other way you could say it is, "that the programmed computer has the right to bring out a particular output." So the ego can say: "I can do what I like" – of course – according to the programming!

A Free Sample

RAHASIA I totally resonate with what you are saying, yet at the same time... maybe I could share something that happened to me. About half a year ago...

RAMESH Your name is?

RAHASIA My name is Rahasia.

RAMESH Do you know what "rahasia" means?

RAHASIA Yes, mystery.

RAMESH Rahasia, what part of the world are you from?

RAHASIA Germany, originally.

RAMESH Ah, your English is quite good.

RAHASIA But I live in Australia now.

RAMESH I see, that is the mystery! The mystery is solved.

RAHASIA Something happened to me last April, which I could call an awakening experience, where since then there is a basic undercurrent knowing that there is no "I", so whenever I close my eyes, whenever I look in, I don't find anybody. Now when I talk about it, I have to say "I" and it's a lie, but if I look in there is nobody and there is a tremendous sense of freedom.

RAMESH How long did the experience last, Rahasia?

RAHASIA Well, there are two things I could relate: there is the experience which is like a curtain opening, and there is a feeling or sensation that everything I see is me, there is no difference. Now this is not happening right now, but there is a knowing about it.

RAMESH Yow mean a recollection of the experience?

RAHASIA No, no, the moment when I close my eyes it is there, there is no "I", there is a sense of "isness" that is part of everything.

RAMESH I see.

RAHASIA So my question is this – I could never call this Enlightenment – but something like an awakening, a call, or something.

RAMESH You know what I call it? A "free sample"!

RAHASIA (laughing)...a "free sample"!

RAMESH A free sample is given, you don't help yourself to a free sample, it is given to you by the Source or God.

Otherwise you could have it every time.

RAHASIA That's true. Yes, it has absolutely been given to me.

RAMESH So, it has come to you by the grace of God, or the Source.

RAHASIA So, when you say there is no individual freedom, I agree with that, yet at the same time there is a tremendous sense of limitless freedom inside. So how does that fit with the idea there is no freedom?

RAMESH So, what you have said, infinite sense of freedom, you have used different words for the same thing. Infinite sense of freedom, are you saying it is contradictory to your experience?

RAHASIA No, not at all.

RAMESH It is the same thing described in different words, a tremendous sense of freedom. Now that tremendous sense of freedom, Rahasia, what is that freedom from? Haven't you ever wondered?

RAHASIA Well, it s a freedom from the "I": the moment there is an "I" thought there is a limitation and where there is no "I" there is no limitation. So I can call it a freedom from the "I".

FREEDOM FROM THE "ME"

Ramesh Freedom from the "me". Quite correct. Freedom from the "me". So what is the "me"? Have you ever wondered? Ego?

Rahasia Ego – as I see it, it is like a collection of conditioning...

Ramesh What you are doing, Rahasia, is describing the ego. But what you mean is the ego: the "me", the ego.

Rahasia But if I really look and try to find it, it is not there.

Ramesh Exactly. That is why several Masters have said this. When the disciple comes in and says: "All I want is my ego to be destroyed", the Master says: "Easy, produce the ego and I'll smash it to pieces." You see? So the ego is a fiction. That is why the "me" is the ego, the thinking mind desiring something, wanting something, thinking how to achieve what is wanted. All that, the thinking mind, is the ego, which is me, which is Rahasia. So what is this ego? Do you think this has to be destroyed?

Rahasia No, it just has to be recognized that it is not there.

Ramesh So, who recognizes? It is the ego who has to recognize that it really doesn't exist. And what is meant by "really does not exist"? *It does nothing!* When can the ego realize that it is really nothing? When it realizes that it can *do* nothing. Why does the ego consider itself so powerful – "I can achieve whatever I want"? That is the ego with a sense of personal doership. So my definition of the ego is not merely identification with one body-mind organism with a name. Many people mistake the ego for mere identification with a body-mind organism and a name. The fact that many consider that as the definition means many egos think that they are only identification with a body-mind organism and a name. And when the Master says Self-realization means annihilation of the ego, the poor ego is frightened: "I don't want Self-realization if it means my annihilation. I don't want to die." You see, that is why the sense of independence you have described, many have said that is accompanied by a sense of helplessness.

RAHASIA Yes, total helplessness.

RAMESH You see, so who feels helpless? The ego. "I don't want to not exist, I don't want to die", and therefore the resistance to Self-realization comes from the ego. What prevents the happening of the total experience? The ego. The ego says: "Self-realization, I am told, means the annihilation of me, the ego, and I don't want to die." Therefore the ego is afraid, the ego resists the happening of Self-realization. Therefore, I tell the ego: "You are not going to die. You have to live so long as the body-mind organism is alive. But with the sense of personal doership destroyed, you will not only live, but you will live a marvelously free and easy life." You see? Then the ego says: "Is that all? I would love that." So how does the ego live a simpler and much easier open life when the sense of personal doership is destroyed? So the ego, according to my definition, is *identification with a name and form, with a sense of personal doership.* So it is not identification which is important, but it is the sense of personal doership. If the Buddha, when he was alive, was called by name, he would respond, wouldn't he, whatever he was called? Master? What was he called?

SWAMIJI Bhagavan.

RAMESH So, if he were called by name, Bhagavan, he responded, didn't he? He responded: "Yes, what can I do for you, my son?" So the fact that the Buddha responded to his name being called obviously means there was identification with a particular body-mind organism and a name. That is why I say that even after Self-realization the identification with a name and form must continue so that the body-mind organism can live for the rest of its allotted span of life. In other words, what I am saying is that it is possible for the ego to live *without* a sense of personal doership, and what is more, to live life much more simply. So what is destroyed by Self-realization is the sense of personal doership. That's all. Life continues to be what it was, according to God's will or the will of the Source and the personal destiny of the body-mind organism.

SWAMIJI Could I elaborate?

RAMESH Yes, of course, any time.

SWAMIJI I'd like to suggest a worst possible scenario just to make my point. I was reading the transcripts of the trial of Rudolph Hoss who was the commandant of

Auschwitz, and in his trial he said in 1944 he was told to wind up the camp. And he said because there was no more gas he ordered the children to be thrown into the furnace without being killed first. He said their screams could be heard all over the camp. So I am suggesting this is the worst possible scenario. How can that be the will of God, how can that be the will of the Source? And you said to me before I don't live my life, that life lives through me. Why would life live through anybody like that?

RAMESH No, that's not your question. Your question is really, basically, "Why does a merciful God bring about an event...

SWAMIJI OK...

RAMESH ...where babies are thrown alive into furnaces?" Is that right? Let's take an extreme scenario...

SWAMIJI Yes, it's an extreme scenario...

RAMESH Agreed, it's an extreme scenario... "Why would a merciful God allow live babies to be thrown into the furnace?" That's the question, isn't it?

SWAMIJI Yes.

RAMESH Now, did God tell you he is a merciful God?

SWAMIJI No, all the pandits did that.

RAMESH God never told you that He is merciful, so you

create a concept of God and you give Him attributes, all-knowing, all-powerful, merciful, then you ask God: "You are merciful, why are you doing these terrible things – handicapped children, disease, war, Hitlers, Stalins, how can you do it?" And God is silent.

SWAMIJI I can't think of an answer to that. I think that is a very good answer. So, one other thing would be, if I do accept on the other hand that it is the will of some Source, then what would motivate me to try to…?

DIVINE HYPNOSIS

RAMESH If you continue to use "me", I shall continue to ask "who is this 'me'?" – and the "me" is an object. Basically, Swamiji, who is this "me"? Who is this "me"? *An object*. We cannot get away from that basic concept. "Me" – who is the "me"? The object thinks there is a "me" because God has created the ego with divine hypnosis. God has created the ego by divine hypnosis which makes the object think he or she is an individual doer.

SWAMIJI *Why?* (with a deep sigh)

RAMESH Because, without the egos interhuman relationships cannot happen.

SWAMIJI Why do they need to happen?

RAMESH Because without interhuman relationships life as we know it cannot happen. The functioning of

Manifestation cannot happen. Having created the Manifestation, the Source has to have that Manifestation function.

SWAMIJI But for what purpose?

RAMESH That's a good question. "For what purpose?" You see, who wants to know the purpose? A *created object* wants to know the purpose, wants to know the purpose or the will of the Creator Subject.

SWAMIJI A legitimate question, surely?

RAMESH I repeat, an *object*. Some time ago, Alexander and his wife Hella came from Vienna. Alexander was out there (pointing to hallway) – he couldn't find a place inside this room. He was a very sincere man but had a strong resistance. So he always had a lot of questions. Hella sat here in the corner with hardly any questions. Then suddenly on the last day she said: "Ramesh, I have one question. I am feeling that what you are really saying is that if I create a painting and in that painting I create a figure, that figure in the painting which I have created can never know why I did the painting." I said: "Hella, you couldn't have put it better." She was delighted. I said: "That is what all I am saying comes to. A created object can never possibly know the will of the creator Subject, and in this case the Creator Subject is Pure Subjectivity, so how can a created object ever know why the subject did whatever it has done?" The second principle is, why did God create this? The point I am making is, Swamiji, life as we know it, the functioning of Manifestation, is based on interconnected opposites: Adam and Eve, good and evil, beauty and ugliness, any number of these interconnected opposites. My point is there never could have been a single moment of life, or the functioning of Manifestation, when only one existed and not the counterpart. It could not be. That is the basis; otherwise it would be a lame manifestation, with one leg. So, the interconnected opposites are the basis of life, and at every moment both have to be there. Therefore, at any moment, Swamiji, my concept is that there have been saints and there have been villains, there has been beauty, and there has been ugliness.

Where the Self-realization has happened, what does Self-realization in effect mean? That the human being, the object in which the Self-realization has happened, remains an object, but *he knows he is an object*. The ordinary man doesn't. So what does Self-realization mean? The realization that the "self" with a small "s" is only an object through which the Source is functioning, and that the functioning means the existence of both the opposites. That is why the sage understands that in life Self-realization does not mean only pure happiness all the time and no pain. That is not Self-realization, and the sage understands that. Therefore the sage continues to live the rest of his span of life accepting that the basis of the functioning of life is duality, interconnected opposites.

And therefore, in the functioning of life, which he cannot avoid, while participating in life, the sage accepts – that is the crucial word, "accepts" – that sometimes he has to suffer pleasure and sometimes pain, sometimes frustration, sometimes satisfaction. So the sage lives life, participates in life, with the understanding that life means duality. So, the sage lives in duality, accepting duality as the basis of life, whereas the ordinary man chooses, judges, one against the other – "I want only the good, not the bad; I want only the beauty, not the ugliness." Therefore he lives not in duality but in dualism. Again my concept. The sage lives in duality, accepting the duality, not choosing one against the other, whereas the ordinary man chooses one against the other and therefore lives in dualism. Choosing one against the other, the ordinary man becomes unhappy. I said beginning with Adam and Eve. Now let me be flippant, Swamiji, and I will tell you a joke about Adam and Eve – nothing that will offend you! So, when Adam was created and the Lord created Eve, Adam was delighted. So, he said: "Lord, why have you created Eve so beautiful, so considerate, so lovely?" So, the Lord said: "So that, my son, you may love her." "And Lord, why did you make her so loving, so much interested in my welfare?" Again, "So that, my son, you may love her." And then Adam said: "But God, why have you made her so stupid?" And God said: "So that she may love you". So nothing that can offend your sensibility. (*Laughter*)

So basically, the sage lives in duality, accepting duality. Accepting duality means living in the present moment, accepting whatever happens. Again, living in the present moment means enjoying life, enjoying life as it happens – sometimes good, sometimes not so good – whereas the ordinary man always wants to have nothing but happiness, which is not possible in the dualistic world. Therefore, the average person is unhappy.

KARMA

> *The doctrine of karma is undeniable, but the theory of the ego has no foundation. Like everything else in nature, the life of man is subject to the law of cause and effect. The present reaps what the past has sown, and the future is the product of the present. But there is no evidence of the existence of an immutable ego-being, of a self which remains the same and migrates from body to body. There is rebirth but no transmigration.*
>
> THE BUDDHA

SWAMIJI What about individual *karma?* Does it exist?

RAMESH *Karma,* of course it exists. That is what life is all about. *Karma* is an action. "Events happen, deeds are done..." The deeds being done is *karma.* But, as the Buddha said: "There is no individual doer." So, *karma* means continuous cause and effect, effect becomes the cause, and further effect. Further effect becomes the cause, and the chain of cause and effect is the continuation in various lives. So my point, Swamiji, is *karma* is cause; that is the basis of life, but there is no individual, there is no individual doer thereof. *Karma,* yes, but not individual *karma.*

ACCEPTANCE HAPPENS

ANADI So, Ramesh, how does the ego...

RAMESH Your name is ?

ANADI Anadi. I am from Canada. So, how does the ego get convinced that there is no individual doership?

RAMESH Very good question. How does the ego come to the final acceptance that he or she is not the doer? That is your question, isn't it? A very good question. The answer is that he doesn't come to the final conclusion. The acceptance happens because it is the will of God.

So, let's go back to why the ego was created. As I explained, the ego was created by the Source because the Source had to create an ego since without the ego interhuman relations wouldn't happen, and without interhuman relations, life wouldn't happen. So the Source, or God, created the ego, and at the same time as part of life, for which the ego was created, the Source also started the process of destroying the sense of doership in a limited number of cases. He created the ego in every body-mind organism and also started the process of destroying the sense of doership in a limited number of egos so that life could still go on. In other words, the happening of Self-realization is part of life. And those few body-mind organisms through which this process of Self-realization has been happening have been created by the Source with such programming that this kind of seeking will happen.

ANADI What about the situation where everybody is Self-realized? Would that be the end of the duality?

RAMESH What it means is the Source is stupid enough to create the egos because life is necessary, and then to demolish all of them, so that life again will stop. So for life to happen and go on, many egos have still to be there. How many, what is the proportion? In the *Bhagavad Gita*, Lord Krishna says that *"among thousands of people, there is hardly one seeker, and among the thousands of seekers, there is hardly one who knows me in principle."* Thousands of people, one seeker, and among the thousands of seekers, one final Self-realization. That's what He says.

ANADI So – not likely – that's the answer?

RAMESH Yes, that's the answer.

SELF-INVESTIGATION: I AM NOT THE DOER

The body is a compound of perishable organs. It is subject to decay: we should attend to its needs without being attached to it, or loving it. The body is like a machine, and there is no self in it that makes it walk or act, but the thoughts of it, as the windy elements, cause the machine to work. The body moves about like a cart.

– THE BUDDHA

~

Eeshwarah Sarvabhootanam Hriddeshe Arjuna
Tishtati /
Bhraamayan Sarvabhootani Yantraaroodhani
Mayayaa//

The Lord lives in the heart of every creature. By
his Maya (divine hypnosis), He causes all beings
to wander through life as though mounted on a
machine.

– BHAGAVAD GITA XVIII /61
~

BOB Ramesh, my name is Bob, from Seattle.

RAMESH You have been here before?

BOB Yes, about three years ago, and three years before that. So, there's obviously a difference between the concept "I'm not the doer" and the realization "I'm not the doer."

RAMESH That's exactly the question where we began. That's the question, isn't it? How does the ego come to the final acceptance that he or she is not the doer? Now, my answer is this – the ego can only come to that conclusion from personal experience. Otherwise, he says: "Ramesh says this, but how do I know it is the truth? Many Masters say that, yet how do I still know it is the truth?" So the ego has to convince himself that he is not the doer. And how? From *personal experience*.

BOB So, when you say "personal experience", what do you mean?

RAMESH *Personal experience* – I mean this: how does the ego come to the conclusion that he is not the doer? *From personal experience!* In fact the only spiritual practice I recommend is what I call "self-investigation", exactly the same thing that Ramana Maharshi called "self-inquiry". I use the word a little stronger: "self-investigation." So who does the investigation? The *ego* does the investigation. How does the ego do this investigation? The only spiritual practice I recommend is that at the end of the day sit back for 10, 20 or 30 minutes and think of one action you are convinced is your action, and after that take as many actions as you like. Then, investigate it thoroughly and honestly, that action which you thought was your action, and find out: "How much control did I have over something which I consider was my action? Is it truly my action so that I had control over it at all stages, or has it really in fact been a '*happening*'?" These are Lord Buddha's words: "Events happen..." Was it only a happening? "I went somewhere, did I go somewhere, what made me go there? I heard someone say something, I saw something, which made me go there, and what I heard or what I saw was not in my control." So, this is investigated on these lines: "After the talk, I went to a restaurant. I went to a particular restaurant – or did I? How did I manage to go to the restaurant? I was hungry, and after the talk several people were talking about going to a restaurant where the food is reasonably clean, reasonably good and reasonably inexpensive. So, why don't I go myself? And so I went to the restaurant. Then I asked for the menu, and from the menu I selected a vegetarian dish. Why? Because I am not a non-vegetarian. Why? Because I can't stand non-vegetarian food. My programming is such that non-vegetarian food makes me ill, I can't even think of it. So I selected a vegetarian dish, and the vegetarian dish which I had selected was not available so I had to take another vegetarian dish. I had to take..." You see, that is what the investigation means. And I guarantee, any action, if you investigate it thoroughly and honestly, you will have to come to the conclusion that there are too many uncertainties, too many improbabilities, too many "it so happened's" for it to have been *my action*. Therefore, it was not my action.

So, action after action is investigated by the ego – *by the ego*, remember – and each time the ego comes to the conclusion: "It was not *my action*". And if this happens time after time, day after day, the ego comes to the conclusion: "What I was convinced was my action turns out to be not my action. In fact, if I were to relate any action, I would probably begin with the words 'it so happened that' – 'I happened to be standing there, *it so happened.*'" So the ego comes to the conclusion action after action: "No action is *my* action". So the ego asks itself: "If so many events have happened, so many deeds have happened, without my being in control at any stage, is the "me" really necessary for actions to happen, is the "me" really necessary?" And day after day the ego, coming to the conclusion that no action is his or her action, becomes weaker and weaker and weaker. That is the big advantage of this practice which I suggest. In the case of other practices, the danger, and I repeat not every time, the danger is that as there is progress, the ego gets stronger. In any system or practice, progress has to be there if it has been done honestly and thoroughly: "I sit in meditation; I sat in meditation half an hour, now I am able to sit in meditation for four hours, and I don't see many people able to sit in meditation for four hours. Therefore, I am superior to others." So there is progress, and the ego gets stronger. That is the danger. For example, *japa*, doing *japa*: "I used to do only 10,000 a day; now I do 500,000 a day. In fact, I think I should keep an account of it so that God doesn't make a mistake."

SWAMIJI Is it useful to investigate while the action is taking place? You have talked about what I would call a "review", and what I am talking about is what I would call "awareness of the present".

RAMESH Yes, if you can do that, by all means. But what is more likely to happen, Swamiji, once you begin the practice, is like this. A few months ago someone who had been in Zen Buddhism for 30 years was here, and he actually said: "I have never thought of this. I started the practice yesterday, and today, by 10:00 this morning every action that happened, I didn't have to wait until the end of the day. Some action happened, and in that moment it came up: 'That action is not my action. That's not my action.' I went to brush my teeth, and while I was doing it: 'I am not brushing my teeth. The brushing the teeth is happening.'" So he said in his case he had to actively do the practice only once. So what you are saying actually happened in his case. While the action was being done, there was the realization, the apperception, that "what is happening is not my action".

SWAMIJI So, are you saying that this would be as good, or better?

RAMESH BETTER! Better for this reason: the ego is not doing it. This experience, this actual investigation is not necessary. The purpose of the investigation is happening, by the grace of God, or the Source.

SWAMIJI You may be interested to know that there is a discourse by the Buddha, where somebody called Bahia asked the Buddha: "How can I be free?" And the Buddha said: *"In the seen, let there be just the seen; in the heard, just the heard; in the sensed, just the sensed; in the cognized, just the cognized."*

RAMESH That's *beautiful!* That's exactly it! In other words, let there be thinking without the thinker, let there be doing without the doer, let there be experiencing without the experiencer.

THERE IS NO INDIVIDUAL EXPERIENCER

There is a state where there is neither earth, nor water, nor heat, nor air; neither infinity of space nor infinity of consciousness, nor nothingness, nor perception nor non-perception; neither this world nor that world, neither sun nor moon. It is the uncreate. That I term neither coming nor going nor standing; neither death nor birth. It is without stability, without change; it is the eternal

which never originates and never passes away.
There is the end of sorrow.

– THE BUDDHA
~

RAHASIA I have a question about this too, because this is how I experience it. I have been with a particular Teacher for twenty years and he defines Enlightenment as when there is absolutely no thought arising in your consciousness. And, if I recall the awakening experience I mentioned earlier or the state which is underlying even today, I am very aware that there are thoughts happening, but I am not the thinker, they are just happening.

RAMESH Quite right.

RAHASIA So, how is your experience of Enlightenment, if you call yourself…

RAMESH The same thing, I told you: *there is no individual doer.*

RAHASIA Yes, but are there thoughts happening?

RAMESH Now, are you telling me that in the case of your Teacher that no thoughts occurred? Would he have dared say that in his case no thoughts occurred?

RAHASIA While he was talking, definitely thoughts occurred; so what I heard him say was, while he was not talking there were no thoughts.

Ramesh What he must have meant, and what you probably misunderstood, was that thoughts may occur but there was no *one* doing the thinking.

Rahasia Well, this I can relate to inside also.

Ramesh There was no *individual* doing the thinking. Thoughts came, thoughts were witnessed. The working mind is working on a job; while he was talking, the talking happened.

Rahasia I travel a lot and I realize each time I get out of an airplane in a different country there are different thoughts coming because the collective thought energy is different so it makes it very obvious it is not my thoughts.

Ramesh That's the point. So what I am saying is this: thinking happens, but there is no individual thinker; seeking happens but there is no individual seeker; doing happens, but there is no individual doer; experiencing happens, but *there is no individual experiencer.*

Rahasia This is a huge relief!

No One Is Doing Anything

Victories over others will make one feel strong. But the understanding that all actions are divine happenings, and not the doing by someone, is a victory over oneself that makes one all-powerful in the peace that follows.

RAMESH So, in the words of the Buddha: "Events happen, deeds are done, but there is no individual doer thereof." So it is only from this personal experience that he has never been the doer, that this understanding can happen. In other words, what is a concept for an ego can become the truth for that ego only by investigation from personal experience that he has never been the doer.

ANADI We are talking about the gradual convincing of the ego. This is still entirely a mind concept, yet at some point it has to become an understanding, you have to see it. And that happens by itself, that is what you are saying?

RAMESH That is correct, it happens by itself, that is what I am saying. The ego says: "If I am not the doer, who is this 'me', is there a 'me' at all?" That is the final question the ego comes to: "Is there a me at all?" And that question can be absolute misery, that question will not let that ego be at all. Every free moment that thought will come, until it becomes the misery of the seeker. And if I had to give it a name, I would say it is "the dark night of the soul". The pain is so deep it becomes almost unbearable and the ego begins to think of suicide, and at that moment, if it is the will of God and the destiny of that body-mind organism, the answer comes from the Source: "My dear child there never has been a 'me' to do anything. You have been suffering unnecessarily. Everything that is done, I do – I, the Source." You see? And then the understanding is final, total.

ANADI Is this "dark night" always a necessary step then?

RAMESH No, not at all. The dark night of the soul has to happen if it is God's will and the destiny of a particular body-mind organism. But, if the destiny of that body-mind organism has never been the strong sense of personal doership, if there has been from the childhood a deep sense of acceptance that all this is happening, no one is doing anything, then there is no question of the dark night of the soul. That again is God's will and the destiny of that body-mind organism.

BHAKTI AND JNANA

BOB So, is there any difference between what you are describing as the understanding that you are not the doer and surrendering to the will of God? That seems like an action, but it's like a non-action at the same time.

RAMESH That is correct. In other words, in this case also it is a surrender, but when the surrender happens, the acceptance happens. Surrender is the word usually used on the path of *bhakti*, of devotion, and acceptance is the word usually used on the path of *jnana*, of knowledge. But, Masters have repeatedly been saying, they are not two. Frankly, what you hear now really honestly proves it. How do I begin? "Thy will be done." What can be more devotional, *bhakti*, than that – "Thy will be done" – no action is *my* action? So I begin with *bhakti*, "Thy will be done", and end up with "I am not the doer", accepting that "I am not the doer". So that way, I begin with *bhakti*, and the *bhakti* ends in knowledge, *jnana*.

Bob So, in one way it is a difference between dual and non-dual thinking – not thinking, but the concept that God is something separate from this body-mind organism and the concept that it's all just one, it's all just happening, it's all just Consciousness.

Ramesh Yes, that's it. "Thy will be done" refers to life as we know it, in the functioning of Manifestation. Finally when we come to the conclusion that life just happens and that no one is doing anything, it ends up with the sense of personal doership being demolished. So if I am not the doer, who does it? – the Source or God.

The Big "S": Source

All things are conditions of mind. That which knows the mind is the unconditional SELF of everything.

Visitor What you call "self" with a small "s", what do you mean?

Ramesh The individual ego.

Visitor And the big "S"?

Ramesh The Source.

Visitor And is it from this world, the Source, or is it the Absolute...?

RAMESH The Source is the *only* Reality, the ONE without the second – Source, from which this Manifestation has emerged. Ramana Maharshi called it "Self" – with a capital "S".

WHAT'S SO FUNNY?

SWAMIJI So, you have had your moment of frivolity, so I am going to take the moment of having mine.

RAMESH Of course! Wonderful! I'm glad – this doesn't exclude frivolity!

SWAMIJI Tell me, what is humor, what makes us laugh, and why is something funny?

RAMESH The point is, that is part of the *programming.* I haven't explained to you what I mean by "programming". By programming I mean this, Swamiji. You didn't have a choice or control over the parents to whom you were born. Therefore you had no control over the genes or the unique DNA in this human object. By the same token, you had no choice about being born to particular parents in a particular environment, in which environment this object has been receiving continuous conditioning from the word go. Conditioning at home, conditioning in society, conditioning in school, conditioning in church or temple. So these unique genes, or DNA, plus this environmental conditioning is the programming, which really decides what you think you like or you don't like. So what you like or don't like is truly not in your control. It depends on the programming.

SWAMIJI So, nothing deeper in the sense of humor?

RAMESH So humor is part of the programming, that's all. You'll even find someone who just can't keep humor out of anything. In fact, it becomes a nuisance. We have a friend, a man called Ed Nathenson, so full of humor and wit. Once, another friend, Heiner, was standing over there and said: "Ed is a wonderful man, but the only trouble is I never know when he is serious and when he is not." And the other thing is, what makes me laugh may not make you laugh. So, the sense of humor itself is according to the programming. Everything is programming. Everything is either programming or the destiny. Destiny is God's will. Programming has also been God's will. So ultimately everything is God's will; and when I say God's will, I mean the will of the Source, or everything happens according to God's will, or the will of the Source, but for the benefit of those who don't like the word "God" I say "Cosmic Law", according to "Cosmic Law."

DESTINY

ANADI You were just talking about predestination. It seems like it would go a long way towards convincing my ego if predestination could be established beyond doubt.

RAMESH You see, all that the ego has to do is to find out from his personal experience, from his *personal experience*. What is your personal experience? Have you had any control over it? Something has always happened.

And, it was not in your control. It was in the control of someone else. But a concept which may appeal to you is that life is nothing but a movie, the movie in which the Consciousness or the Source has written the dialogue, a movie which has been produced and directed by Consciousness, *Consciousness is playing every character in the movie*, and it is Consciousness which is witnessing the movie. And the movie is already there. We can only see it bit-by-bit. *But the movie is already there.*

RAHASIA I recently had a very convincing experience of this. I went to one of those *naadi* readers in the south of India.

RAMESH The most convincing proof you want is a *naadi* reader. Yes.

RAHASIA It's all written there even thousands of years ago, even the names of my father and mother and when I was born.

RAMESH Their names were there? Then that is a genuine one. But many get fooled. I always say the nadi must tell you your name and twenty other names.

RAHASIA It was mind-boggling.

RAMESH It is mind-boggling, but that is the conviction he wants.

ANADI I am a physicist by training and predestination seems to go against very fundamental things shown by physics. So, that is why I am struggling with this idea.

Ramesh Yes, but as I say, everything is a concept. Take the nadi reader – you heard what he just said. Those names were already there, even two thousand years ago, carved in the papyrus leaf, before ink and paper were discovered. That establishes the time frame – those names were already there.

Anadi Yes, this certainly should be proof.
Ramesh You wanted proof, this is the kind of proof that can be given.

Anadi But otherwise, this predestination, is it something that you perceive directly, or that you know that is true from your own experience?

Ramesh As far as I am concerned, I had that total conviction as a child that whatever is going to happen to me has happened, and no one has the power to change it. It had its good points in this way: with that conviction I didn't have to do any boot-licking in my career. I knew if I were going to have a promotion, no boss could stop it. And, if I were not going to have the promotion, no amount of boot-licking would produce it. So the advantage was, for example, that if my superiors wanted some opinion, I gave it to them, and they knew that the opinion would be based on what I felt and not on what I thought they would like to hear, and frankly most of them liked and appreciated that. So this conviction has been there from the very beginning.

Anadi So, you were born with that conviction. That's not much help to us!

Ramesh No. No, it isn't. But, I would say you were born with this excitement of needing proof!
(*Laughter*).

∼

Everything happens altogether by itself.
The shadow of causation can never be caught because
all things and events are merely interconnected
differentiations in form of a single, unified field.

— RAMESH BALSEKAR

∽

EVENT 2

~

REALITY –
THE UNBROKEN WHOLE

What is physical reality? The manifest universe. But physicists tell us that no object exists unless it is observed. This would mean that the manifest universe exists only as the functioning of it, and the functioning of the Manifestation is life as we know it. Life as we know it depends entirely on interconnection: interhuman relationships, which cannot exist unless the interconnected opposites exist at the same time – male and female, night and day, likes and dislikes, good and bad...

Modern physics tells us that access to the physical world is only through experience. In other words, one could say that external reality is nothing other than our interaction with it. This is a fundamental assumption of "complementarity", a concept developed by Niels Bohr to explain the wave-particle duality of light: wave-like characteristics and particle-like characteristics are obviously opposites, but both of them are necessary to understand light, although of course they cannot exist at one and the same time. Does this perhaps mean that life cannot exist without interconnected opposites?! Does it also perhaps mean that life can exist only through experience, and that a human being cannot exist without interconnected qualities of head and heart existing at the same time, in the principle of complementarity? What is experienced in the interhuman relationships is only one aspect of the complementarity at any time, but both aspects must exist.

Is a particular human being a "good" person or a "bad" person? It would depend on with whom he experiences life. Light behaves like particles or like waves, depending upon the particular experiment that is being performed. In other words, both the complementary aspects of light are necessary to understand the nature of light, and it is meaningless to ask which one of them really is light.

The programming in every human body-mind organism contains both the aspects of being human – good and bad – and it is meaningless to ask whether a particular person is a good person or a bad person. It would depend upon "what experiment is being used", which person he or she is interacting with, in the existing circumstances – the experience.

There is another important aspect to the matter of experience, and that is that actual experience is hardly ever restricted to merely two possibilities – either/or, guilty and innocent, good and bad, true or untrue... This either/or is an illusion "caused by assuming that experience is bound by the same rules as symbols." While in the world of symbols (material things taken to represent immaterial or abstract things), everything is either this or that, there are more alternatives available in the world of experience.

There is a story of a visiting American being stopped by a group of masked gunmen during the Lebanese civil war. It was for the American a critical situation in which one wrong word could have cost him his life. The masked gunman asked him: "Are you a Moslem or a Christian?" For a moment he was speechless. Then, by the grace of God (irrespective of whether God is Moslem or Christian!), the fear of life suddenly broke through the illusion of the symbolic "either/or", and he found himself saying: "I am a tourist."

It would seem that an integral part of quantum mechanics is the recognition of the quality of experience that transcends the logical restriction of the symbolic "either/or". Experience is a state of being; the description of a state of being is a symbol, a concept – they do not follow the same rules.

The more one studies the conclusions of modern physics, the more one begins to see the intrinsic closeness between modern physics and the Eastern philosophy, whether Buddhism or Hinduism. Modern physicists have just realized what the Eastern mystics had realized hundreds of years ago: in order to understand Reality, one necessarily has to cast off the bounds of the concept and symbol in order to experience or perceive directly the "inexpressible nature of undifferentiated reality." In other words, the "undifferentiated reality" is the same reality of which we are all born a part of, but seen in a totally different way by the ordinary person and by the Enlightened mystic.

The physicist has now begun to see the reality as it has been seen by the mystic: there is only one unity; all the seemingly different parts of the universe are manifestations of the ONE whole, united reality. The physicist has found that something need not be either a wave or a particle; it can be both, a *wavicle*! He also has found that any subatomic particle *anywhere in the universe* "knows" what is going on anywhere else. Subatomic particles constantly seem to be making decisions based on decisions made elsewhere at the same time. Indeed, the physicist has come to the conclusion that the quantum particles may not be particles at all!

A subatomic particle cannot be viewed as a thing, as an object. Quantum mechanics see subatomic particles as "tendencies to exist or happen," expressed in terms of probabilities. This would seem to mean that it could perhaps be meaningless even to speculate upon what "thing" a subatomic particle is. Could it be that the physicist is coming to the conclusion which the mystic had always known: the ultimate "stuff" of the universe is a no-thing, an illusion?!

In other words, it would seem that quantum mechanics is coming to the conclusion that the universe is not a collection of separate parts, that the separate parts, including the human beings, do not exist independently of one another but are actually parts of "one all encompassing organic pattern."

Again, it would seem that the quantum physicist has come to the conclusion that the future of physics must depend on his altering fundamentally his own thought processes concerning the view of reality, bringing them more in line with those of the mystic: the reality of concepts and symbols is an illusory reality, even though we have to live in that illusory reality. Thus the science of physics and the phenomenon of Self-realization or Enlightenment may not be too far apart! Both have come to the conclusion that an experience and a description of that experience – the experience (the experiment and the result of it) and its description through symbols have a totally different set of rules. Happiness cannot be described, it is an experience; electricity cannot be described, it is what it does.

The mystic finds problems explaining what Enlightenment is; the physicist finds problems trying to explain subatomic phenomena. *Neither can be visualized.* The difficulty persists for the physicist whether he uses the common language or the mathematical analysis – both are based on concepts and symbols. In other words, both for the mystic and the physicist, the problem is not in the language; the language (with its concepts and symbols) is the problem.

What it all boils down to is: mind (the realm of thought processes and symbols) cannot be used to understand reality. Mind has to be transcended. Reality has to be "experienced", not "understood". Mind can be used only to the extent of understanding that what is sought to be understood is beyond the "understanding" by the individual seeker. There can only be an impersonal awareness of reality as manifested in the universe – no part can understand the unbroken wholeness: "That-which-is", here and now.

According to the physicist David Bohm: "We must turn physics around. Instead of starting with parts and showing how they work together (the Cartesian order), we start with the whole." Also, "Parts are seen to be in immediate connection, in which their dynamical relationships depend, in an irreducible way, on the state of the whole system (and indeed, on that of broader systems in which they are contained, extending ultimately and in principle to the entire universe). Thus, one is led to a new notion of *unbroken wholeness*, which denies the classical idea of analyzability of the world into separately and independently existing parts…"

Separate parts together constituting physical reality was the basis of classical science, which was only concerned with how these separate parts are related. Since then, the physicists have now come to the conclusion that it might not be possible to construct a model of reality. This indeed means an acknowledgment, a recognition, that mere knowledge by itself cannot lead to the understanding of reality. What the "Copenhagen Interpretation" brought out is that "the proper goal of science is to provide a mathematical framework for organizing and expanding our experiences rather than providing a picture of some reality that could lie behind those experiences."

In 1964 Dr. J. S. Bell published mathematical proof of a strange "connectedness" among quantum phenomena, which since then has come to be known as Bell's Theorem. The Theorem, which he reworked and refined over the next ten years until its present form, in its implications is generally considered as perhaps the one most important single work in the history of physics. Bell's Theorem points directly to the experience of Enlightenment in the Eastern spirituality! Physicists subsequently have "proved" rationally that our rational ideas about the world we live in are grossly deficient.

According to Bell's Theorem, the principle of local causes is false. The principle of local causes expounds, quite simply, that what happens in one area is quite independent of what happens in a distant separate area. The failure of this principle of local causes means, again very simply, that what happens in one area does indeed depend upon what happens in a distant separate area. This means that we live our lives "in a nonlocal universe ('locality fails') characterized by superluminal (faster than light) connections between apparently 'separate parts'."

Almost everything in physics has rested upon the assumption that nothing in the universe can travel faster than the speed of light. One can therefore imagine the turbulence that has been caused by Bell's Theorem.

It is rather a coincidence that only about fifteen days ago (May/June 2000) there was a general report in the media that research has revealed that energy has been discovered which travels faster than light – perhaps even 300 times faster than light! If this is confirmed, one can imagine that the physicist is not too far away from the Eastern mystic. Would it not also suggest that the past, present and future are all there like a completed movie?

What the acceptance of Bell's Theorem does is to project the "irrational" aspects of subatomic phenomena directly onto the macroscopic realm. As Henry Stapp has said: "Our ordinary ideas about the world are somehow profoundly deficient *even on the macroscopic level.*" This means that Bell's Theorem has turned our common sense into nonsense. This proposition that information is transferred superluminally (faster than light) has been "proved" rationally by quantum physics.

In other words, one would have to accept that events as autonomous happenings is an illusion. As David Bohm has put it, one is led to a new notion of *"unbroken wholeness."*

The demolition of locality would seem to lead us to the conclusion of a "superdeterminism": "free will" is an illusion and *there cannot be any such thing as "could this have been avoided if..."* This simply means that there could not have been any possibility of our doing anything other than what we *are* doing this moment. Perhaps we could put it this way: whatever is happening at any moment through any human being is exactly what is supposed to happen – according to the Cosmic Law, based on the unbroken wholeness. And no human being, a created object in the Manifestation, can possibly know this "Cosmic Law". This is how the Hindu principle of non-duality, *Advaita*, would see it.

It is interesting to note that according to managerial practice in Japan, only the minimal time and effort is spent on who was guilty for what happened. The effort is concentrated on how to prevent the same mistake occurring again in the future.

It would have to be admitted that only a profound and penetrating intellectual quest, transcending all rationality based on concepts and symbols, into the ultimate nature of reality could bring about a quantum leap ending in the ultimate wisdom.

There is a peace invocation which precedes the *"Eesha"* and other Hindu *Upanishads*, which perhaps says it all:

Purnam adah purnam idam
Purnat purnam udachyate
Purnasya purnam adaya
Purnam evavashishyate

The invisible (Brahman) is the Whole;
The visible (the Manifestation) too is the Whole;
From the Whole (Brahman), the Whole
(the visible universe) has come.
The Whole (Brahman) remains the same,
Even after the Whole (the visible universe) has
come out of the Whole (Brahman).

So, one must ask: Do the subatomic particles really exist? They don't move in space and time, they don't carry mass, they don't have charge, they don't have energy in the usual sense of the word. Perhaps they are a subatomic illusion in the illusory universe!

∼

Event 3: Part 1

~

All the elements of being, both corporeal and non-corporeal, came into existence after having been non-existent; and having come into existence pass away.

There is not a self residing in Name and Form, but the cooperation of the conformations produces what people call a man. Just as the word "chariot" is but a mode of expression for axle, wheels, the chariot-body and other constituents in their proper combination, so a living being is the appearance of the groups with the four elements as they are joined in a unit.

There is no self in the chariot and there is no permanent individual self in man.

– The Buddha

~

The Human Computer

Thinking Mind And Working Mind

RAMESH So, Swamiji, after yesterday's talk, do you have any comments?

SWAMIJI I was interested in your making a distinction between "identification", which you felt was something that didn't have to be dealt with, and "doership", what you call "doership". Could you further elaborate on the differences between them? I take identification to be a feeling that certain given experiences or objects *"am I "*.

RAMESH Yes, sure. There's a book you can take a copy of before you leave, *The Infamous Ego,* where I refer to this. The main distinction I make is this; another distinction I like that goes along with it – I repeat again, it is a concept, *it is a concept,* that the mind I divide into the working mind and the thinking mind. The thinking mind is the ego. The working mind is not concerned with what happens in the future about the job that is being done. That aspect of the mind which deals with the job at hand, whatever it may be, it may be planning, or it may be the actual task at hand whatever it is – that is what I call the "working mind", which continues after the sense of doership is gone. In the case of a sage, identification with a name and form continues with the working mind. It is the thinking mind, the ego, which is concerned not so much with the efficiency of the work taken in hand, but almost totally with the consequences of the work for itself. The working mind is concerned only with doing a good job. The thinking mind says: "I don't care whether the job is good or not, if it brings me the results I want." The thinking mind is concerned with the consequences, the results in the future; the working mind is not concerned with the future. Both the thinking and working mind dip into the memory. The thinking mind dips into the memory and projects its wants and desires into the future, and its fears. The working mind dips into the past only for the experience. Let me give you an example. The surgeon has a body before him, and he has to make an incision. So, the working mind dips into the past: "From my past experience, which is the best place to make the incision?" Based on his experience, he decides which is the best place to make an incision. This is the working mind, dipping into the past memory, the experience. So the working mind dips into the past memory, but it ends in the present moment of doing the job. The thinking mind goes into the past, but it projects its fears and hopes and ambitions and consequences into the future. The working mind is not concerned with the future. And the thinking mind is the ego. You see? So that is an essential part of the difference between the sense of doership and the mere identification with a body-mind organism. Ramana Maharshi lived 50 years after his Self-realization, so for 50 years the body-mind organism lived in society and had to participate in life, limited, yes, but still participated in life. Ramana Maharshi had to suffer pain, and Ramana Maharshi also felt responsibility. He said once: "I left my mother and my brother as part of the *samsara*, and now, (referring to the ashram) I left a small place, and look what I have got now."

SWAMIJI Could we say in his case, or in the Enlightened person's case, he would still have the thinking mind which functions but there is no concern, or he doesn't take it seriously any longer? Let's say that those desires are there but one doesn't react to them, or do they cease completely?

RAMESH Let's stick with these desires. What happens to a sage? Desires arise, anger arises, fear arises, compassion arises, and all these that arise are the outputs because of an input. Yesterday we didn't go too much into this. What is the input that the Source uses to put in any human computer, uniquely programmed human computer, to get a specific output from a specific human computer? That's what has been happening with the billions of human computers: what the Source, or God does, is to bring out a unique action, a unique output, through every body-mind organism. In other words, an action that happens at any moment could not have happened through any other body-mind organism. It had to have a particular uniquely programmed computer for that output to happen. Now, that body-mind organism could be that of an ordinary man or that of a sage. If they are similarly programmed, a similar output must arise. Let us say, there is a sage – and there have been plenty of sages with short fuses – where anger would arise quickly; plenty of sages especially in the Hindu mythology. There are plenty of sages where anger would arise, and along with it a curse. Now, whether you would call such a sage a sage is immaterial. That is a technical matter, another matter. He was a sage. So whether it is a sage or an ordinary person, anger can arise, fear can arise, compassion can arise. So, if the same reaction can happen because of the same input, then where is the difference? Where is the difference between an ordinary man and a sage if both see the same thing and anger arises in both, or fear arises in both, where is the difference? According to the Buddhist understanding, what would be the answer, Swamiji?

SWAMIJI I can think of one sutra where somebody asked the Buddha...

RAMESH... unless you say that is not possible. What I am saying is the *sage* cannot be afraid, the *sage* cannot be angry. Then we are on a different basis altogether.

SWAMIJI That would be the Buddhist position.

RAMESH But more practical would be what I say?

SWAMIJI I know what the Buddha said, so I am interested in what you say. I am interested in you. In one place somebody asked the Buddha: "An ordinary person feels pain and an Enlightened person feels pain, so what is the difference between them?" The Buddha says: "*When an ordinary person feels pain he then laments and beats his breasts and falls into despair. He is like a man who, on being shot with one arrow, is then shot with a second arrow. But the Enlightened person on feeling pain does not lament and cry and beat his breasts. He is like a man on being shot with one arrow is not shot with a second arrow.*" That would indicate the idea that the Enlightened person...

RAMESH... has control?

SWAMIJI A Buddhist would say there is no reaction, he sees it as an illusion or as not real, and therefore how could fear arise?

RAMESH But Swamiji, Christ on the Cross, he shouted

out in pain, didn't he?

SWAMIJI I didn't think he was Enlightened.

RAMESH But the Pope recently said, if you remember, the final salvation can only happen through Jesus Christ. And yet here you are saying that Jesus Christ may not be Enlightened! Anyway, so my explanation for the shouting out is this: pain can arise and pain can make the body-mind organism shout out in pain.

SWAMIJI I see a difference between that and, say, anger. Say somebody attacks me with a knife. I feel that I am threatened, so if there were no "I" where could fear arise from?

SWAMIJI You see, fear arises, according to my concept, from the programmed computer.

SWAMIJI Conditioning?

RAMESH Conditioning and genes, both…

SWAMIJI So it would be a biological function…

RAMESH It is indeed a biological, mechanical, function. The arising of pain, the arising of anger, the arising of fear, is automatic, mechanical. The real point is what happens after that.

SWAMIJI OK.

RAMESH That is the difference between the ordinary man and the sage. Fear arises; at the moment the arising of fear is a mechanical, or as you say, biological happening. What happens after that, that is where the difference comes in. The ordinary man says: "I am afraid." What has happened? Fear has arisen. The ordinary man says: "I am afraid. I don't want to be afraid. I want to be strong and brave like my friend. I don't know what to do. This is what happens every time. Something happens, and I tremble with fear." That is the involvement in horizontal time. The arising of the fear in the moment, then the involvement of the ordinary man, "I am afraid", that is where the sense of doership comes in and takes him into a horizontal involvement, so that he is unaware of the next moment or the next ten moments or the next twenty moments – because he is involved in horizontal time. What happens to the sage? He witnesses the fear arising.

SWAMIJI In other words, there is some standing back from it, he sees it as an event?

RAMESH No. Then, the witnessing of the anger, you can say, is by the ego, but in the case of the sage there is no sense of personal doership. So the arising of the fear is witnessed, but there is no sense of personal doership in the ego to take delivery of the fear and to say "I am afraid." There is no "me" as the doer. So, my concept is, the sage witnesses the fear; not only does the sage witness the arising of the fear but also the resultant action. The arising of the fear and the resultant action are one in the moment. The body-mind organism may run away. So what the sage sees is the arising of the fear leading to that body-mind organism running away, whereas his friend, sage or not, accepts the fear and does something about it or gets involved. So, the fear arises, the sage runs away. Now, the sage running away: it is not really the sage running away but the arising of the fear, and the reaction of the body-mind organism with its self-protective reaction. With this self-protective instinct, the body runs away.

SWAMIJI Once again, the biological reaction…

RAMESH It is still one mechanical reaction. There is a story about Adi Shankara, the original one who got all the Advaita together. His basis was that life, or the Manifestation, is an illusion. So the king sent for him and listened to his talk. Then the next morning what the king did, knowing Adi Sharkara's routine, that Shankara at a particular moment would be at a particular spot crossing a fairly broad road, was to go and wait at some distance with his elephant chariot. As Shankara was crossing the road, the king asked the chariot driver to charge at him. Shankara ran across the road and took shelter. Later the king sent for him and said: "Look, this morning, such-and-such a thing happened." Shankara replied: "So what's the problem?" And the king said: "You ran away." "So", Shankara said, "in that illusion which is life, in that illusion you charged at me as part of the illusion, and my running away and taking shelter was also part of the same illusion. That also is part of the same illusion."

So what happened? The arising of the fear and the instinct to protect itself – the body-mind organism ran and took shelter. Therefore, you can't say Shankaracharya ran.

Therefore, if Ramana Maharshi during the night could be heard moaning from his cancer, or Ramakrishna Paramahamsa really shouting: "Mother, why are you making me suffer like this?", or Jesus Christ: "Father, why hast thou forsaken me?", it is the pain taking further process of shouting. So, the shouting may happen, running away may happen, but it is seen as part of a *happening* through a body-mind organism that is his. In other words, if the arising of fear and running away happened in some other body-mind organism, the sage would witness it without any reaction to that natural reaction. So, the arising of the fear and the running away happen not through some other body-mind organism, but through this body-mind organism. Where is the difference? My point is, it is the sense of personal doership in an ordinary man which gets him involved. In other words, the ordinary man reacts, or the ordinary man's ego reacts to the natural reaction, the biological reaction, or mechanical reaction, you see, whereas in the case of a sage, since there is no ego with a sense of doership, there is no reaction to the biological reaction. That is the difference.

THE PROGRAMMING OF THE HUMAN COMPUTER

It may seem shocking that the human being, who is supposed to have been created "in the image of God", is being reduced to a programmed computer.

SWAMIJI That is very clear. Now, may I ask this?

RAMESH Please.

SWAMIJI I can understand how, when a person becomes Enlightened, the biological conditioning continues no differently from before. That is very clear. In the case of what you called an "input", or "programming"...

RAMESH Let me make it clear. I probably didn't make it clear. What is the input? A thought comes. Generally, a man says: "I had a thought." But what has happened is you don't have any control, nor does any sage at any time have any control, over the thought that comes next. The thought that comes next comes from the pool of Consciousness, or God sends it, you can say in simpler terms. That is the input. The next thought that comes, over which you have no control, is the input, or similarly what is seen next or what is heard next or smelt next or tasted next or touched next; any of the senses, which of the senses will next react to what object, no one has any control. That is the input. A thought, something seen or heard, over which you have no control, that is the input. And the reaction is also something over which you have no control, because that is according to the programming. And by the "programming" what I mean is this: nobody had any choice over the parents to whom he or she would be born. Therefore, no one had any control over the genes or unique DNA in every human body. By the same token, no one had any control to be born to particular parents in a particular environment, in which environment the human object received its conditioning from day one – conditioning at home, conditioning in school, conditioning in society, conditioning in church or temple, continuous conditioning. And what is this conditioning? This is right, this is wrong; this is fair, this is not fair; this is good, that is bad; you should do this, you shouldn't do that. Basically, that is the conditioning on which is based your judgment at any particular point, and the decision you make about any particular problem that arises.

SWAMIJI   So, could we say that externally we can't see a difference between the sage and the un-Enlightened person?

RAMESH   That is correct.

SWAMIJI   None at all?

RAMESH   None at all! That is why I keep on repeating it is a concept, because it is a concept. That is my concept. My concept is that the immediate arising as an output for an input over which I have no control, the reaction is because of the programming, genes or DNA plus environmental conditioning, over which also I have no control. And that is the same for a sage or anyone. It is a body-mind organism, a mechanical piece.

SWAMIJI   In the case of the biological conditioning, I can see that that couldn't change. In the case of the psychological input or conditioning, which you would equate with the thinking mind, I could see, for example, a person feels pain and they groan. But in the case of, say, a kleptomaniac, there seems to be an element of choice there, and I therefore would assume there may be some difference between the Enlightened person's behavior and the un-Enlightened person's behavior...

RAMESH... which difference comes in as a reaction to the biological reaction. That is exactly the difference that I am saying is between a sage and an ordinary person. But that difference is located in the reaction of the ordinary man to the biological reaction. In the case of a sage, because the ego with a sense of personal doership is not there, there is no subsequent reaction of the ego to the biological reaction.

SWAMIJI So there is some difference, or there may be some difference, in their behavior.

RAMESH Oh yes, indeed, indeed, but not in the natural biological reaction. That is what I am saying.

ROHIT In the case of a sage, after the incident of a fear, a registration may not take place. For example, in the example you gave of the king, the person would not have any grievance against the king who tried to curse him. Is that the difference, a registration does not take place? He does not keep on thinking that this event may happen or this may not happen, so he is free from it instantly.

RAMESH That is what the thinking mind is. That is why I say the sage lives in the present moment, while for the ordinary man, because of the involvement in horizontal time, for the ordinary man the next few moments are gone. So the involvement of the ordinary man is not there in the case of a sage, and the involvement is due to the ego with a sense of personal doership.

ROHIT   But why does the registration not take place because of the way the mind is here? The moment there is some event or some impression or something, the mind immediately absorbs it and reacts.

RAMESH   The mind which reacts is the thinking mind, which is absent in the case of a sage. It is indeed the thinking mind that does the reaction to the natural biological reaction. It is indeed the thinking mind that is the ego, which reacts to the natural reaction, which is exactly what is absent in the case of the sage. It is the thinking mind with a sense of personal doership: "I am the thinker, I am the doer, I am the experiencer, I am the seeker" – that is the thinking mind, the ego with a sense of personal doership. That being absent in the case of a sage, a reaction to the natural reaction doesn't happen. In the case of an ordinary man, the ego reacts to the original reaction, and continues to react.

SWAMIJI   And we can assume that you are making this distinction between these two for the sake of clarity, not that there are two quite separate minds. These are just different functions of the same mind?

RAMESH   Yes. Sure. That is why I say that *conceptually* I divide the mind into two aspects: the working mind which continues in the sage even after Self-realization, and the thinking mind, which is the ego, more or less living in the future and worrying and planning about its future, which is the ego with a sense of personal doership. Therefore, what I say is the "me", the "thinking mind", and the "ego with a sense of personal doership" are different names for the same thing – they are synonymous for the same thing: ego with a sense of personal doership. The "me" in the case of a sage – the sage is not worried about using the word "me", or "mine". Why? Because there is the total understanding that the "me" and "my" words have to be used in order to communicate. But as far as he is concerned, he knows that the "me" and "my" words refer only to the body-mind organism.

God Is A Concept

SWAMIJI What about this? Yesterday you were talking about doership and you were also talking about the "Source", what you call the "Source". When you are talking about doership and absence of this, I can understand how you can speak from personal experience. If that has happened, one would know. But when you are talking about the function and what-have-you of the Source, how do you know that? Is this from *sruti*, or from experience or…

RAMESH That is a concept. The basic concept is that there is some Reality, there is some *Reality*; everything we perceive with the senses is unreal. So, before the Manifestation occurred there has to be what I call the Source: that is the basic concept. Whether you call the Source Emptiness, whether you call it Nothingness, or whether you call it Noumenon, or whether you call it Primal Energy, or you call it Consciousness, is immaterial, because there has to be a Source from which this visible Manifestation has emerged.

SWAMIJI So you have introduced this concept to make it clearer, to explain things…

RAMESH Yes.

SWAMIJI I see, this is very interesting. I am happy to hear that.

RAMESH It is a concept, it is a *concept*. That is why, Swamiji, you must have heard me say at least a dozen times, "this is a concept", "this is my concept". And I have made it clear, according to my concept, anything any sage has ever said at any time is a concept. Anything that any scripture of any religion has said at any time is a concept. A concept is something that some may accept and some may deny. The Truth is only that which no one can deny, because it is not liable to interpretation.

SWAMIJI In other words, it is a direct experience?

RAMESH Yes.

IMPERSONAL AWARENESS OF BEING

SWAMIJI When you are talking about doership, you are speaking from direct experience. And when you are talking about the Source, you are speaking purely conceptually.

RAMESH That is correct.

SWAMIJI That's wonderful; I like that!

RAMESH That is indeed correct, and I am so anxious that this is not misunderstood that I keep repeating that anything anybody has ever said is a concept. So someone may say: "Even Lord Krishna?" – I say of course! So the only Truth is the *Impersonal Awareness of Being*, the *Impersonal Awareness of Being, Existing*, I AM. I AM is the only Truth which no one can deny. Someone, an atheist, will come to me and say: "Look Ramesh, I have been at it for twenty years, I've got a doctorate in Comparative Religions, and I honestly believe that God does not exist." So, I would say God is a concept, created by the human mind, so you are entitled to say that God does not exist. But whether God exists or not, can you deny that you exist? Not you as so and so, but the *Impersonal Awareness of Being*? Can you deny that? No one can. And that is the only Truth; and what is more, the moment we talk about it, it becomes a concept. You see?

SWAMIJI I do, I do, I do.

ROHIT You talk about "beingness" being the Truth. But beingness has its own time limit. After some time it vanishes.

RAMESH No. Beingness can never vanish. You, individually, personally, may be unaware of it. That is why I say "*Impersonal Awareness*", which is usually hidden or covered by the individual awareness.

ROHIT Is it what Nisargadatta Maharaj says about the

Absolute that you say is the *Impersonal Awareness*?

RAMESH Yes, yes.

ROHIT And on top of it is sitting this impersonal awareness of I AM – because at times he refers to "I Amness" as being a concept, as Consciousness, as being a fraud. Is it personal Consciousness which he is talking about being a fraud?

RAMESH Yes.

ROHIT It is not the other one?

RAMESH That is correct.

There Is No Doer, There Is No Experiencer

An ordinary person undergoes experience, while the Self-realized one is the experience itself.

RAMESH Yes?

BOB Ramesh, it seems like that sages not only have the awareness of "I am Brahman", but they seem to go into states of absorption, or *samadhi*, in which they lose personal consciousness and they seem to identify with the Source at that time. And they come out of that and someone can again say "Ramana" and they will turn around and look. So it seems that that's beyond just the sense of personal doership or not; it really is identification with the Source, it would seem.

RAMESH No. Even that, you used the active form and therefore the problem. What did you say? "Ramana Maharshi goes into...". Ramana Maharshi did not "go into"; the going into *samadhi* happened. And that is true meditation. True meditation is that which happens, not something which somebody does, even if that somebody is Ramana Maharshi. In fact, Ramana Maharshi would say to the question: "Do you do meditation?", he would say: "I do nothing." The answer really would have been "I do nothing."

BOB Right. Well, he would talk of something like *sahaja samadhi*. He would call it the natural state.

RAMESH So, you are thinking of someone going into *sahaja samadhi* by doing this. I would say *sahaja samadhi* happens, and *sahaja samadhi* is a label given to an experience.

BOB ...which I am assuming an individual is having.

RAMESH That is the problem.

BOB That is the problem! So your concept is that no individual is having this experience of *samadhi*, because the very experience I am describing is losing individuality!

RAMESH That is why I keep saying: "Thinking happens, there is no thinker; the seeking happens, there is no seeker; and seeking is doing, therefore doing happens and there is no doer. Experiencing happens, there is no experiencer." Now, an indication is this: an experience has happened, and it's gone. For Ramana Maharshi, it would never even cross his mind: "I would like to have that experience again", whereas the ordinary person who has the experience says: "I would like that experience again."

SWAMIJI So it would imply that the more you try, the further away you get?

RAMESH I agree: that is exactly what is meant! The more you try – I'll give you an example, but it probably won't be one that concerns you. Have you ever played cricket or baseball or anything?

SWAMIJI Absolutely not. (*Laughter!*)

RAMESH That is why I dared to say that you are probably not concerned with this! But anyone who has played a ball game knows there is someone hitting the ball, the batter, and another catching the ball, the catcher. So, I am talking of the catcher. The thinking mind is anxious – "This is a crucial catch: if I catch it, my side will win, and if I drop it, my side will not win." He's anxious, and the anxiety may make him go forward to catch the ball. But if there is nothing very much hanging on it, he will just wait for the ball to come into his hands. And there will be a save, and the commentator will say: "The ball was safe in the hands of the experienced fielder." And the experienced fielder is exactly this – he knows that if you try to get it, you will lose the ball. And, take a simpler experience at home: someone goes to visit a friend and he hasn't been there for a long time. In the meantime a child has appeared and while he is sitting in the living room, the child comes around and the child peeks. If the person goes and tries to catch the child, the child will run away almost always. But if the person sits there and smiles at the child, the child will go away and come back in a minute. He will come a little more forward. So the person smiles again. And if he has something with him, a sweet or something, all he has to do is sit quietly and offer it. The child comes closer. So if the person does not show any anxiety to grab the child, I am almost certain that the child will come nearer and nearer and before he knows it the child will be in his lap, accepting and licking the lollipop. And, another example in practice: several people have said that Vaslav Nijinsky, the famous dancer, is reported to have said: "I dance best when Nijinsky is not there." Singers say: "I sing best if I am not there" – in Indian classical music, when the musician gets up you see him almost coming out of a trance.

SWAMIJI Is that the working mind?

RAMESH You could say that is the working mind from this culture. But actually it is in neither. You could say the working mind starts the process, the working mind starts the singing, the working mind starts the dancing; but when it ends, even the working mind is gone.

SWAMIJI So that comes back maybe to what you were saying yesterday, when you were saying there is only one spiritual practice that you would recommend and that is what I called "reviewing".

RAMESH Yes, self-investigation.

SWAMIJI Then I say what about the ability to be aware as things are happening, investigating as things are happening? Could you talk more about both of those?

RAMESH Yes. You see what happens is, the length of the spiritual practice is totally out of the practicer's control – and whether the practice is started or not is God's will and the destiny of the body-mind organism. How quickly the experience happens is also God's will and the destiny of the body-mind organism. But if the final acceptance happens, that "I am truly not the doer", then the result of that total acceptance is that things are happening and they are merely witnessed – witnessed not as "my" doing.

JANE My first question is about this: it seems like a lot of my time is spent in thinking about the future. In other words, planning, having a calendar, and figuring out, etc., etc. So how is it possible to do all that and stay in the present?

RAMESH So, how can I live my life efficiently without planning – that's your question, isn't it?

JANE In other words, I am scheduling events for six months for people ...

RAMESH So, can we not bring it down and focus the

question? "How is it possible to live one's life without precise military-like planning, to live an efficient life?" That's the question, isn't it? So, that planning which is done is by the working mind. The working mind does the planning. Then the thinking mind says: "Hey, you've got a plan, but how do you know it is going to work?" That is the thinking mind. The working mind plans and the thinking mind grasps doubts about what may happen in the future. You see, there is the working mind and there is the thinking mind. There's a comic strip in the States, Mutt and Jeff. So, they are going in a car up a hill. Mutt is the driver, and with body language coaxes the car to go up the hill. When he reaches the top, Mutt gives a big sigh of relief and said: "If we hadn't reached all the way to the top, we would have slid right back to the bottom." And Jeff says: "No, Mutt, we wouldn't have, because I had the handbrake on full." (*Laughter!*) So, the foot on the accelerator is the working mind, and the pulling the brake is the thinking mind, which stops the working mind from working efficiently. So the thinking mind is always the handbrake.

JANE I have one other question. You know, we have two teachers. You are one of our teachers, and our other teacher says do practices, do sadhana. So it feels like we are kind of caught in the middle. Any advice?

RAMESH Sure. Which concept you will accept is God's will and your destiny. You have two concepts. One gives you freedom and the other gets you involved. So which one you will accept will depend on God's will, which has already been working through your programming, you see. Whether you will be able to accept it or not depends a lot on your programming. And even that is ultimately God's will and the destiny of that body-mind organism. I've seen people the very first day totally receptive: "I know I am not the doer, not because Ramesh says so, but I know from personal experience. I have done the investigation into my personal happenings, and therefore I know from my personal experience, I have come to the conclusion that I am not the doer." Otherwise, the final acceptance may have happened, but you will never know, you will never know whether it is the final acceptance or whether it is still an intellectual acceptance. That you will know only after the investigation.

ROHIT So is the investigation necessary?

RAMESH I think it is necessary, let us say, for most people.

ROHIT I have felt that listening has made me stop this investigation and personal meditation. Not that I don't sit – I sit whenever I feel like it and sitting happens for more than half an hour. And one doesn't even know.

RAMESH Yes, so what is your question?

ROHIT Not another question, but just out of curiosity I would like to share. I was thinking that in your teaching as compared to the *Bhagavad Gita* there is no distinction between *asuri sampati* (demonic trait) and *daivi sampati* (godly trait).

Ramesh Why do you say that?

Rohit You say they are the opposite side, the reverse of the same coin.

Ramesh So whether *asuri sampati* happens, or the *daivi sampati* happens, who is in control of that? Are you?

Rohit Well, then I wanted to investigate it further, and I went into the Chapter 16 which deals with the *asuri sampati* and the *daivi sampati*, and surprisingly the first characteristic of the *asuri sampati* that is the demonic characteristic, is *ahamkara*, and that led me to see the dictionary definition of "ego". And surprisingly, I have never looked into the meaning of "ego" in the dictionary, and it was very interesting. "Ego" is according to the Oxford Dictionary conscious thinking subject as opposed to non-ego or object.

Ramesh Fine, a conscious thinking object believing that he is doing the thinking.

Rohit Therefore every functioning of the ego is in the triad: the thinker, the thinking and the object thought about.

Ramesh That is correct.

The Ego Of The Sage: Only The Ash

Rohit Now, as the sage you say only the sense of

personal doership is not there. You say the sage has an identification as far as a name and form are concerned, and he responds. But, when a sage is called by his name is it the ego that responds?

RAMESH The ego responds, yes Rohit, but not with a sense of doership

ROHIT Is there any ego?

RAMESH Yes.

ROHIT Is this triad then there?

RAMESH The triad is not there. The triad is concerned with the sense of personal doership, not with the ego. The triad is concerned with the sense of doership.

ROHIT Is there then a subject?

RAMESH There is an ego that enables the sage to live in society with a working mind. For fifty years after his Self-realization, Ramana Maharshi, speaking to someone used the words "I" and "you". The sage speaks to someone and uses the words "I", "me", "mine" and "yours".

ROHIT But that is not the functioning of the triad, it is not a subject functioning?

RAMESH That is what I am saying. Therefore, the sage lives in society, and while living in society an ego is necessary, and what is not necessary is a sense of personal doership. Therefore, ego is mere identification with a name and form, which is the ego without the sense of personal doership. Ramana Maharshi gives a beautiful example. He says: "The ego of a sage is like the remnants of a burnt rope." A rope is burnt: is the rope there? Yes, but what is there? Only the ash.

ROHIT But the ash does not exist as the rope.

RAMESH That is exactly what he said. Therefore the ash which remains is not to be used to tie up anybody. The ego of the sage is totally harmless. It is merely "like the remnants of a burnt rope." So, what is burnt out in the case of a sage? A sense of personal doership. The sense of personal doership is burnt out, annihilated. And yet, what enables the sage to live fifty years after Self-realization is mere identification with a name and form together with the working mind.

ROHIT Would it be correct to say that appearances appear before the sage and appearances appear before an ordinary person, and the ordinary individual takes the appearance, takes delivery of it and considers it real, but appearance as far as the sage is concerned is always an appearance and he is aware that it is only the functioning of Consciousness?

RAMESH That is exactly what I would say, yes.

CONDITIONING

SWAMIJI Could I just ask for clarification on something

you were saying? With somebody who hasn't reached the state of Enlightenment, new conditioning is taking place, whereas somebody who has reached a state of Enlightenment or non-doership, no new conditioning is occurring, but they still have previous conditioning which means they respond in a certain way to certain external stimuli.

RAMESH That is correct: the previous conditioning is usually the basic conditioning. But mostly what the sage reacts to is not so much the conditioning, as the genes or DNA. Now the scientists ascribe almost everything to the genes. You are a timid man – genes; you are a drunkard – genes; you are unfaithful to your partner – genes; you are a homosexual – genes. So in the case of a sage, what responds to the input is mostly the genes. But it is part of the programming.

SWAMIJI But no new conditioning is taking place?

RAMESH No, no new conditioning is taking place, because the new conditioning would always refer to the ego accepting what it says, or to the thinking mind. But what is happening here is new conditioning, the effect of which may be to alter or amend the existing conditioning. But since in the case of a sage no doubts remain, there is no room for conditioning to take a seat.

SWAMIJI So, spiritual practice is really trying to change one's conditioning and put in a different conditioning?

RAMESH No. The spiritual practice that I am talking

about is to annihilate the sense of personal doership. You come to the total irrefutable conclusion that no action has been my action, no action is my action, no action will be my action. Not only is no action my action, but no action is anybody's action. Indeed, all action is a divine happening through some human body or another. No action is something done by someone. My action is not my action; your action is not your action. All actions are brought about by the Source or God through each human computer by the way it has been programmed. In other words, therefore, life flows. The individual ego tries to swim against the current, and becomes unhappy. In going with the flow, the pain may be there, which is participation in life.

So it is not that the sage doesn't experience pain and pleasure – he does. The sage experiences pleasure, certainly. The sage is hungry and you give him a good dinner, he will be happy, he will be certainly pleased. So, in the Hindu philosophical jargon, the sage is the *bhogi*, the enjoyer. Strictly, the understanding is: "*Twam eva karta, twam eva bhokta*"; "Thou art the doer, Thou art the enjoyer." But in the body-mind organism, the input of a good meal brings up the pleasure. But that pleasure which arises in the case of a sage – he is called not only a *bhogi*, but a *maha bhogi* – "super-enjoyer", the sage is called a super enjoyer. The sage is called a *maha bhogi*, why? For this reason: I get a meal and I am really satisfied. I am not thinking of an earlier meal that was slightly better than this. I am not wondering whether I shall ever have a meal as good as this. The enjoyment of that meal is pure, without being diffused by the thinking mind. So the enjoyment is total. That is why he is a *maha bhogi.* It is not diffused by the thinking mind.

SWAMIJI And the pain he would also experience is basically just at the biological level?

RAMESH That is correct. In fact, that is a good question, Swamiji. When my Guru, Nisargadatta Maharaj, towards the end of his life was in great pain with cancer, he would perhaps moan; a moan would come out of the body. So somebody asked, out of great sympathy: "Are you in great pain, Maharaj, are you in great pain?" And the answer which promptly, spontaneously came out: "Yes, there is great pain."

∼

EVENT 3: PART 2

~

IS ANY ACTION MY ACTION?

*There is rebirth of character, but no transmigration of a self.
Your thought-forms reappear, but there is no ego-entity
transferred. The stanza uttered by a teacher is reborn in the
scholar who repeats the words. Only through ignorance and
delusion do men indulge in the dream that their souls are
separate and self-existent entities.*

*This body will be dissolved and no amount of sacrifice will save
it. Therefore, seek the life that is of the mind. Where self is,
truth cannot be; yet, when truth comes, self will disappear...
In the truth you shall live forever. Self is death, truth is life.
The cleaving to self is a perpetual dying, while moving in the
truth is partaking of Nirvana which is life everlasting.*

*Where does the wind dwell? Where does wisdom dwell? Is
wisdom a locality? Is there no wisdom, no enlightenment,
no righteousness, and no salvation because Nirvana is not a
locality?*

– THE BUDDHA

~

THERE IS NO QUESTION OF A SIN

*You cannot commit a sin, nor a meritorious deed, of which
the Lord takes note. The light of the basic knowledge is
covered by the darkness of the ego's delusion, and thus the
individual thinks in terms of sin and merit.*

– BHAGAVAD GITA V/15

∼

TORE In my Christian world, under your theory that none
of the actions are mine, none of the actions are yours,
how do I explain then sin, and in Catholic terms, mortal
sin? Surely, there must be something better than that I
am just swimming against a stream?

RAMESH You see, according to my basic concept,
no individual does any action. All action is a divine
happening through that particular body-mind organism,
because it is God's will and the destiny of that body-mind
organism. So if an action happens through this body-mind
organism, I accept it as God's will, and the consequence of
that action goes with the action. So an action happened
because it is God's will, and the consequences, good,
bad or indifferent, are also God's will and the destiny of
this body-mind organism. Therefore, according to my
basic concept, there is no question of a sin, original or
otherwise.

TORE But that's why Jesus came here, to rescue us from
those.

RAMESH Oh is it, did he? Did he tell you that he has come here to rescue you from sin? You see, it all comes right down to the bottom line. The bottom line is: "Is it my action or is it not?" See from your experience: "Is it my action or is it not? Then, if it is not my action why should I feel proud or guilty, whatever the consequences?" So now, if an action happens through this body-mind organism called Tore which hurts me, knowing that no action can be *done by Tore*, I also know if I have been hurt it is because it is God's will and my destiny. If I am hurt, it is because I was destined to be hurt. If it happened through a body-mind organism called Tore, or if it happened through a body-mind organism called Nord, it is irrelevant. Therefore, knowing that it is not Tore's action which has hurt me, how can I ever hate Tore?

TORE Well, that's both comforting and scary.

RAMESH You see, that means, knowing no action is my action, there is no question of pride or guilt, or sin. Knowing that it is not anybody's action, there is no question of hatred or envy or jealousy about someone, you see.

TORE That is a wonderful thought.

RAMESH That is what happens in the case of a sage where this understanding is total. Pain and pleasure happen, but not pride or guilt. Hurt happens, but not hatred, you see. So the sage participates in life, very much so, and therefore he is liable to get pain, pleasure, or whatever, to what degree is God's will and the destiny of the body-mind organism of the sage. Some sages may be programmed, destined to have more pain than someone else or more pleasure than someone else, so he accepts it as the destiny of the body-mind organism. No question of pride or guilt or hate or envy. That makes life simple though not necessarily easy: whether it is easy or not depends on God's will and the destiny of that body-mind organism. That is what I mention, that it may not be easy. Someone got a bit fed up by my saying that life need not be easier, and he came with a bit of anger. He said: "Ramesh, you keep on repeating life does not necessarily get easier, but in my case it has been easier." He explained that he is in marketing, and since this understanding has become deeper and deeper his business has been thriving. So, he said: "How can I say it doesn't get easier?" I said: "The answer, my friend, is this. What has happened is, or what the immediate effect of this total understanding is – even intellectual understanding – the immediate effect is that the thinking mind interferes with the working mind less and less. That means the thinking mind allows more and more the working mind to function more efficiently, and if the working mind functions more efficiently, why should there not be more rewards?" For him the working mind did happen to function more efficiently, so he could say: "Now I go to my customers and I seem to be talking with a certain amount of ease, which is appreciated by my customers. Earlier, the customer may have had some doubts." The feeling of the customer was: "How do I know that Avinash is really telling the truth?" Earlier, he was only concerned with his business and his commission, and now what comes out is so relaxed that the customer doesn't have that doubt. He said that he got his business more and more easily, and his commission was more and more. He said: "So to that extent life for me has been easier." That is why he didn't like me to say that life may not be easier. So there is a logical scientific explanation for it, and that is, that the thinking mind, the handbrake, is not on. The thinking mind interrupts the working mind less and less and therefore the working mind functions more efficiently thereby getting more rewards.

It's Not Your Responsibility

FIONA Saying that all actions are happening *through* the person means I am not the doer. So my question is about personal responsibility.

RAMESH Now, personal responsibility, what do you really mean by "personal responsibility"? "Responsibility" is just a word, you see, and your real question, I think is: "If this is truly accepted by me, will it not make me an irresponsible person?" Right? Is that your basic focused question?

FIONA It is. I could just go around saying: "This is happening through me, I am not doing it."

RAMESH Yes. The point is, this responsibility, so far you have not accepted that you are not responsible for your actions, so have you been acting with total responsibility, Fiona? Can you put your hand on your heart and say: "All of my actions have been totally responsible"?

FIONA No, I can't.

RAMESH Why?

FIONA A lot of it is just unconscious...

RAMESH Exactly! Therefore, about responsibility, my point is, being responsible, acting in a responsible way generally, or not acting very responsibly in a general way is part of the programming. So, whether this acceptance is there or not, whether you act responsibly or not, and to what extent you act responsibly is part of the conditioning. So if you are programmed to act in a very responsible way, making sure that you are not hurting anybody, that what you are doing is right, then what you are saying is, Fiona is someone who is programmed to do what she thinks is right and fair. And she is worried that she may not be able to do that any more. So, if that is the conditioning, if you are very responsible, do you think that this conditioning will suddenly make Fiona irresponsible? It can't. On the other hand, if someone is born to be irresponsible, I am not saying that this acceptance is going to make that person more responsible.

FIONA Would you say that sages are responsible?

RAMESH It depends on their programming. Now, a person who gets angry very quickly is irresponsible. If he were totally responsible and in control, he wouldn't get angry, but he does get angry, some more than others. Nisargadatta Maharaj had a short fuse – he would get angry very quickly. But, the important point about the anger is, in the case of a sage anger is momentary. In the next moment he is again open to whatever happens. One moment anger, the next moment the sage is open to whatever the moment may bring. I'll tell you what happened once in the case of my Guru. Somebody asked a question, and anger flared up. He said: "You have been coming to me for six years and you ask a stupid question like that?" Anger. But that person who asked the question knew Maharaj, and he said: "Maharaj, what can you expect out of a damned fool like me?" Everyone laughed, and Maharaj's laughter was the loudest. In the case of an ordinary man, what is likely to have happened? He would say: "That man made me angry. Therefore I shall not laugh at his joke." So, Maharaj was present moment-to-moment. One moment anger, the next moment laughter, and the third moment maybe compassion. You see?

HARDAN Why did Ramana Maharshi run away when he came out of this period of just lying in the cave, two times coming from the cave he tried to run away from the seekers?

RAMESH Because the programming was that at that moment he didn't care for company, so in the body-mind organism, you could say fear arose. But, because it was God's will and the destiny of that body-mind organism to be of great help to thousands of people, the body-mind organism began to accept whatever happened and the fear receded. Anger, now there is a misconception because people saw Ramana Maharshi quiet and very peaceful; they never saw him angry or ruffled. So they thought that was the effect of Self-realization. It wasn't. That body-mind organism called Ramana was programmed from the very beginning to be quiet and unruffled, not to be angry, accepting whatever comes. That was the natural programming of that body-mind organism. If that misconception is kept, someone would say: "That man gets angry, how can he be a sage? How can he be a sage? I have seen him being afraid, so how can he be a sage?" So, when you think of an individual doing something as a sage, then there are problems. But if you see something happening as part of the programming of this body-mind organism, then many of these questions and problems don't arise. Programming of the body-mind organism of the sage would include sexual tendencies as part of the genes. There's a story I heard from a person who was himself concerned. He told me he was in the inner circle of a quite well-known Guru, and being at the higher level he could go anywhere without anybody's permission. And he told me this himself. He once found his Guru with a young boy. So it so startled him that he left the door open and ran away back to his room to pack his bags to leave, and then he thought: "I should at least tell the Guru why I am leaving." So he went to the Guru, and the Guru of course knew. He said: "I am going." And the Guru said: "All right, go", but the words he added and which were repeated to me by the same man were: "Don't forget, you have created the problem and you will have to solve it." Those were his words, as repeated: "You have created the problem; if you want to go, go, but remember you have created the problem and you will have to find a solution."

BOB If you eliminate the sense of personal doership, do you also eliminate selfishness or self-interest?

RAMESH No, because that would be part of a natural tendency, based on the programming, you see. So something arises, selfishness, the ego wanting to do something for itself, will not be there. But preferences...

BOB What I mean is you are in a situation, say you get the food or someone else gets the food.

RAMESH Then more than likely the tendency would be for the sage to offer it to someone else. And in fact, there is a photograph of Ramana Maharshi feeding the monkeys.

FIONA So, I am still on the story of the sage with opening the door and finding the sage with a little boy. I have heard stories like that from people who have been very affected, seemingly quite traumatized, by the event. So, back to the idea of personal responsibility, there is no responsibility on the part of that sage?

RAMESH So, the person who is affected traumatically by the incident has seen the incident from the point of view of personal responsibility. And that is precisely what this Guru said: you have created the problem because you have been thinking from the point of view of personal responsibility. And there is no personal responsibility here: an action has happened. If the society and the law consider that action bad and illegal, that action will have consequences, and this body will have to bear those consequences as part of its destiny. What does the sage see? An action has happened, and it may have bad consequences. Bad consequences happen, not necessarily every time, but bad consequences do happen. But if bad consequences do happen, then the sage accepts it as part of his destiny, part of God's will. An action happens, my destiny; and consequences happen, also my destiny.

FIONA So that is to say that the sage could just as easily be sexually abusive as anyone else?

RAMESH If that is the programming in that body-mind organism, to that extreme, but the body-mind organism which is programmed to do the spiritual seeking is unlikely to be excessively programmed in a particular way.

SWAMIJI In relation to this particular incident, if the sage were caught like that and the police did come, then he would just go to prison and take the humiliation?

RAMESH Exactly. He will accept the act as God's will and the consequences also as God's will. And you say he will go to jail – yes, he'll just go to jail!

SWAMIJI And there would never be the point where he would say here is the young man I am very interested in, and the consequences of getting caught might be horrendous, therefore I am going to make an act of will and avoid this.

RAMESH That is the thinking mind – it's not there.

SWAMIJI Whatever would happen, would happen...

RAMESH That is the basis. Now, take a specific case from 60 to 70 years ago. Ramana Maharshi died in 1950, which is already over 50 years. Sometime before that, the practice in Kerala in south India was for all respectable women to go about with their breasts open, bare. And it was considered that only a woman of loose virtue covered her breasts, in order to advertise that she is available. So at that time a young man came to Ramana Maharshi, obviously extremely sincere and probably emotional and he said: "I am newly married, I am deeply in love with my wife. But the young lady who is a neighbor affects me deeply. Her breasts excite me and I am worried that I may commit adultery. Please tell me what I should do." So Ramana Maharshi's answer was surprising, and for that answer I am assuming that Ramana Maharshi was deeply impressed by the sincerity of the man, the young man saying : "I am recently married, I am in love with my wife, and I don't want adultery to happen." So he said: "You are always pure." And, he didn't stop there. He added further: "Even if adultery happens, do not think about it." And this particular incident is not to be seen in all the books written about Ramana Maharshi, because many writers would say: "Oh, I can't put that in. It will be interpreted as 'Ramana Maharshi condones adultery.'" But there was a report with all of the details: "Even if adultery happens, you need not get involved in it personally." So, if adultery is to happen, it is the destiny of two body-mind organisms concerned, whatever be the consequences. But, it may not happen. So what subsequently happened, I don't know. Maybe the neighbour was married off and everybody was happy.

SWAMIJI So really what you are saying is that if somebody were to say that is a very explosive doctrine because it could be misused terribly, what you are saying is that if people are going to misuse something terribly, they are going to do it no matter what anybody says.

RAMESH That is precisely correct, Swamiji.

SWAMIJI So, nothing will make any difference, if one fellow wants to interpret what you say in that way to have a great time, nothing will make any difference, he will, whether you said it or not.

RAMESH That is correct. It is conditioning. And here, there is fresh conditioning. And how this fresh conditioning is going to affect the existing conditioning in whichever body-mind organism, frankly I don't know, and I am not interested.

SWAMIJI It's not your responsibility...

RAMESH It's not my responsibility, absolutely.

SWAMIJI And there is nothing you can do to change it anyway.

RAMESH That is correct.

TORE You are making me a little nervous...

RAMESH I can imagine, I can imagine.

TORE... I guess, because I live to believe that I can be a better person tomorrow than I am today, except that the operating system was programmed by God, but I would hope that I have some way of influencing, of putting in a better software system every day.

RAMESH So, you can pray to God. You can pray to God that he makes you a better person. But whether that prayer is answered or not...

TORE So He would change the operating system, if He wants.

RAMESH If He wants, that's the point. If He wants. But, what did you say, it frightens you, or makes you nervous? Now tell me, why does it make you nervous? Because you don't know what is going to happen tomorrow! If you are not in control of your life...

TORE YES!

RAMESH "I don't know what I will do tomorrow! If I am not in control of my life, I don't know what I will do tomorrow." So far in your life, Tore, have you ever known what you are going to do tomorrow?

TORE No. No. But sometimes my thinking mind is better than my working mind.

RAMESH That is the point, the thinking mind, *the thinking mind*: "I want only the good things." And if you are a good man: "I want only just what is not necessarily only good for me, but..." And, Tore, the most magnanimous thing you can do is to say: "I want that to happen which will be best for humanity." And Tore says: "I am such a great man, I am thinking not for me, but for the whole of humanity. What a wonderful man I am." That is what the ego says. With this understanding, the human being always thinks of humanity as the most magnificent, and therefore he says: "I am such a good man, I think of humanity." So, my point now, Tore, is this: as the smallpox germ was eliminated, the human being was magnificently proud – "No more children will be affected by smallpox. It is a wonderful thing that has happened. And the one who discovered it, I hope he got a good reward." Now, my point is, what about the whole happening from the point of view of the smallpox germ? The smallpox germ is as much a part of the Manifestation as the human being. So what happens and how many units are affected, is again God's will.

ROHIT In the case of a sage, is it not a freedom from all the conditioning and all the desires? What happens with the dissolution of the ego, doesn't it affect his body-mind mechanism also, and how would he commit adultery in that case?

RAMESH That is the whole point. That is what Ramana Maharshi says: "*You* will not be committing adultery." That is the point – because *you* can do nothing! No action is *your* action.

ROHIT What I am saying is in the instance you gave where some Guru was having some inappropriate relationship, he would not be a Guru if indulging in this. He has no freedom from his conditioning, no freedom from the desires.

RAMESH That is so. What is your understanding about Enlightenment or Self-realization?

ROHIT It is freedom from all the conditioning and freedom from all the desires.

RAMESH And that does not happen. So your understanding of Self-realization is totally different from what actually happens. So, the understanding of someone else may be that only he is Self-realized who is able to walk on water. If you are not able to walk on water, you are not Self-realized. Or, a sage with Self-realization should not suffer pain because he is Self-realized. That is not true. Many sages have died in great pain. It is really your understanding of what Self-realization is.

ROHIT But doesn't a sage make a very deep inquiry into life and very deep inquiry into why there is suffering and pain in this world? And he discovers first-hand that the main cause of the misery in the world is the conditioning of the mind. And he becomes so sensitive that the conditioning in some cases dissolves, and he brings a message of compassion and love. So, sir, isn't it a truth that freedom from conditioning only can bring compassion?

RAMESH Freedom from conditioning, nobody can get, nobody can achieve. Conditioning which has been created by God or the Source, no one can change it.

Rohit But, you know, God may have willed it in some cases. In some sages it will be dissolved!

Ramesh Then it will be dissolved because it is God's will and the destiny of that body-mind organism. But if it is not to be dissolved, it will not be dissolved.

Rohit But, if it is not dissolved, he is not a sage! Can we not say, sir?

Ramesh So, with all desires gone, I doubt if you will find a single sage!

~

*Discrimination between the interconnected opposites
into which the Source has extended itself, through
space-time, is the conceptual bondage. Acceptance
of the duality of the interconnected opposites in the
conceptual universe means transcending the conceptual
universe – Self-realization, Enlightenment, Awakening,
the end of bondage.*

– Ramesh Balsekar

∾

Event 4

~

Consciousness Is All There Is

What sudden Enlightenment indicates is the mending of the dichotomy of the whole mind, whereby the division of the mind into subject and object no longer prevails. Then there is no subject perceiving an object: no "me" perceiving and judging a "you". There is only the happening of a perception without judging, a mere witnessing.

Huang Po: "A perception, sudden as a thought, that subject and object are one, will lead to a deeply mysterious wordless understanding; and by this understanding will you awake to the truth of Chan."

Enlightenment is not any alteration in our state; it is only a sudden disclosure of our state, of what we have always been, and not realized: pure Subjectivity.

Impersonal Awareness

RAMESH A physicist and a Buddhist monk make a great

combination! (*Laughter!*) Yes Swamiji, this is your last day, I am told.

SWAMIJI Yes it is.

RAMESH So have you got your list of comments?

SWAMIJI I do have.

RAMESH Let's go through them.

SWAMIJI You have used three terms: Consciousness; mind, in the sense of working mind and thinking mind; and also one that particularly intrigues me, Impersonal Awareness of Being. Would you talk about the distinctions, if any, between them?

RAMESH *Consciousness is all there is*. Consciousness is the only Reality.

SWAMIJI But not in the sense of the Berkelian philosophy.

RAMESH No – Consciousness is the only Reality in whichever sense. In fact, just yesterday I read that in the Indian scientist community they are going to create conditions half a second after the Big Bang. What struck me afterwards was this – would they be able to create conditions half a second before the Big Bang?! So, Consciousness-at-rest is what is, conceptually, half a second before the Big Bang. Half a second after the Big Bang Consciousness-at-rest became Consciousness-in-movement. Potential Energy activized itself.

SWAMIJI I know this is a difficult term, but when I think of Consciousness in the Western sense, say William James, Consciousness is "to be conscious", that is, to see, hear, taste, touch and smell. You do not mean it in this sense?

RAMESH "To be conscious": to be what, Swamiji? Consciousness – you are trying to describe Consciousness by saying "to be conscious". To be what?

SWAMIJI Well, I am conscious of you, I am conscious of seeing, of feeling, or, there is consciousness of...

RAMESH In other words, if there were no consciousness, you wouldn't be able to see me, or to hear me, I wouldn't be able to see you or hear you. The primal base is Consciousness. Consciousness is the only Reality. Consciousness-at-rest is Potential Energy. After the Big Bang, the interpretation is that the Potential Energy has activized itself and the Potential Energy, in order to be potential, has to activize itself some time. Otherwise, Potential Energy would be dead matter. So, that is why I say that it is the nature of Reality to create the Manifestation. It is the nature of the Potential to activize itself some time. It is the *nature of the Potential* to activize itself, otherwise the Potential would be nothing, it would be dead matter, and it is Consciousness-at-rest which is the Potential Energy. Consciousness-in-movement is half a second after the Big Bang. But, the important thing so far, Swamiji, is that there is Consciousness-at-rest and Consciousness-in-movement, where there is awareness of itself – that is, where there is an Impersonal Awareness of Being. Consciousness-at-rest, when there is no awareness of being, and Consciousness-in-movement, when there is this Awareness of Being, are the same Consciousness. They are not two.

SWAMIJI Give it to me again.

RAMESH Consciousness-at-rest is the same Consciousness which is in movement. Swamiji who is sitting down is the same Swamiji who is standing up, or lies down, or runs or walks. So, *Consciousness is the only* Reality in whatever aspect. Consciousness-at-rest is what is before the Big Bang, and Consciousness-in-movement is what is after the Big Bang. It is only after the movement begins when there is Awareness of Being. Otherwise there is no necessity of any Awareness of Being.

SWAMIJI So, when it is the Awareness of Being, what is the "being"?

RAMESH Being is Potential Energy, which can only exhibit when it is in activization. Therefore, Potential Energy, Consciousness before the Big Bang, is something no one can know, because that is all there is. How can anyone know Subjectivity as such? Pure Subjectivity – how can anyone know that? In fact, the Pure Subjectivity doesn't even have to know itself. Not until the Potential Energy activizes is it aware of the energy. Consciousness only in movement is aware, *I AM*; that is Consciousness. Consciousness in action through an individual body-mind organism, through a sentient being, is mind. Consciousness in action through a particular body-mind organism, through any of its senses, seeing, hearing, touching, or whatever, is Consciousness in action. If there were no Consciousness, the senses wouldn't work. For the senses to work, the aspect of Consciousness, conceptually, is called "sentience". So we say there is a sentient object and an insentient object. So, Consciousness-in-action is the sentience in a sentient being. And the sentience in a sentient being is the mind – the totality of the mind which I conceptually divide into the working mind and the thinking mind. That is the conceptual framework which is a pointer to the Truth. So far as the human being is concerned, which is a sentient being in action, its thinking, the mind, can only go back to its Source, which is Consciousness-in-action. Consciousness-in-action means the Awareness of Being, and that awareness of being is of the Consciousness through whichever body-mind organism Consciousness becomes aware of itself, it is the impersonal Consciousness. But when the Consciousness identifies itself with a particular body, with a sense of personal doership, the Impersonal Awareness becomes personal awareness, and that's where the trouble starts. So the real Self-realization is to be able to go from the personal awareness to the *Impersonal Awareness*. The personal awareness sees or hears or judges and acts. So when this sense of personal doership is gone, then what remains is really the Impersonal Awareness, with a working mind which enables that body-mind organism to continue to function for the rest of its span of life.

SWAMIJI So the spiritual practice that you were talking about is to enhance the possibility that the Impersonal Awareness of Being will occur more frequently?

Ramesh   Yes, that is the practice, that is what happens during the practice. The personal awareness is the ego with a sense of personal doership, which frequently clouds the Impersonal Awareness, the true peace. The personal awareness, the identity, the ego with a sense of personal doership is what interferes with the natural peace. Impersonal Awareness means peace. What normally happens is that the personal awareness which is there most of the time doesn't allow the basic peace of Impersonal Awareness to be. So as the understanding goes deeper through this practice of self-investigation, the happening of the personal awareness interrupting the peace of Impersonal Awareness becomes less and less and less. The interference becomes less and less and the happening of the peace, the Impersonal Awareness, becomes more and more.

Swamiji Now we have a practice, that is in Buddhism… You have a practice which I will call "reviewing", that is at the end of the day you are thinking back, investigation…

Ramesh   Just a minute – I say, "at the end of the day" to begin. But if you are in the happy position of being able to take a few minutes off your normal work and do the investigation, nothing prevents you. In fact, that is what happens as the practice becomes deeper; invariably, the working mind tries to find gaps during the working day when this investigation can happen. So, in the beginning, at the end of the day, and then at a certain time, maybe the next day or two or three days later you see it happening during the middle of the day between two bouts of work.

There is a sudden realization that what I thought I was doing was just happening. A flash of the result of the investigation without the investigation!

SWAMIJI Now this is very similar, or it seems to me, to what we call *vipasana*, but the emphasis is not so much on seeing the impersonality of doership, but as seeing the impersonality of the discrete experiences.

RAMESH Repeat that please, Swamiji.

SWAMIJI So in our practice, it seems to be very similar, but the emphasis is not so much on seeing the impersonality of doership, but on seeing the impersonality of the discrete experiences; so one becomes aware or mindful just of the fact of seeing, just of the fact of having a feeling, or something like that. What do you think of that?

RAMESH You see, the basis is this: *who* does the practice, *who* wants Self-realization, *who* wants Enlightenment? The ego!

SWAMIJI So what you are saying is to just let it happen rather than to try to do it.

RAMESH No, let the ego investigate it, let the ego investigate from his or her own personal experience in order to come to the conclusion, and the ego will say: "I have done the investigation, no one else, I myself have investigated a number of actions which I thought were my actions and each time I have come to the conclusion that it was a happening, not my doing." So it is the *ego* which comes to the conclusion from personal experience that it doesn't exist as a doer, that it just doesn't exist.

ELIMINATION OF THE "ME"; OR, ALL THERE IS, IS UNICITY

> *The death of the me-doer revives the subjective "I". The removal of the pseudo-subject, the obstruction, reveals the Source, Pure Subjectivity, in all its splendour.*

SWAMIJI That is very clear to me. What I am now asking is, rather than in the case of doing, what about in the case of just experiencing, which seems to be the emphasis in the Buddhist practice, just seeing experience as a discrete reality that arises and passes away?

RAMESH In that case, *who* is looking for what?

SWAMIJI So, you would get *beyond* the experience to *who* is looking at the experience?

RAMESH Yes. And perhaps because this aspect is lacking, that people have confessed to me that he or she has been doing *vipasana* meditation for thirty years, and the question comes up: "When am I going to get what I am supposed to get?"

SWAMIJI Yes, it is a problem, it is. (*Laughter!*)

RAMESH Isn't that your …

SWAMIJI No, no, I agree...

RAMESH After twenty years, thirty years: "When am I going to get what I am supposed to get?" Here, for the ego, the aim is limited, the aim is limited to only finding out whether he or she is the doer of actions which he or she thought he or she was before. And the ego comes to the conclusion: "I have personally investigated – it's not a concept from somebody – and I have come to the conclusion from personal experience that none of the actions which I have so far investigated – and it's quite a few – not a single one could I truly and honestly accept as my action." Then the ego asks: "Who is this *me* who is so concerned about it? Is there a *me* at all?" And this the ego finds to be an extremely painful process, in some cases, or in some cases not at all. So in those cases where the resistance is programmed to be at the high level, this intense misery becomes the "dark night of the soul".

SWAMIJI Well, you might be interested to know that in the Buddhist analysis, it says that before the experience of Enlightenment there is an experience called *nibido*, which means "the horrors".

RAMESH That's it! You called it "the horrors", I called it the "dark night of the soul" because that expression has been familiar to me. But that is it, "horrors"; only when the investigation reaches that stage of horror or impossibility and the ego is almost ready to commit suicide, then the question doesn't have the quality of an intellectual question because of this horror. The question assumes absolute utter pain, and therefore the question is asked not by the ego intellectually, but the pain, the horror, is felt in the heart. In other words, the question is originally started by the ego: "Is there an actor, is there a doer, is there a 'me' at all?" And finally the question gets asked from the heart, which is the Source, so the question: "Is there really a 'me' if the 'me' is not doing anything and I know from personal experience that I am not doing anything?" – then the question gets asked not from the intellectual level, but from the heart which is the Source. And when the question gets asked from the Source, the answer comes from the Source: "My dear child, there never has been a 'me' to be unhappy. All action is a happening created by me, the *I*, the Primal Energy, the Consciousness, the Reality." And then there is no question. The answer comes from the Source. And that, the answer coming from the Source that there is no individual doer, that there never has been, is itself, according to my concept, Enlightenment or Self-realization. The answer coming from the Source, that "other than 'I' there never has been a 'me'", the answer from the Source, that *"other than I, there never has been a 'me'"* is, according to my concept, Enlightenment or Self-realization, which means the elimination of the "me", of the ego as the doer.

So the ego continues to live thereafter, after Self-realization, merely as identification with a name and form, still different from the other appearances as an individual entity. To that extent there is separation. So, there is bound to be separation in the world of duality, so long as the body-mind organism is alive and functions in duality. When the functioning is in duality, separation must exist.

But separation to what extent? Separation such that I am one object, and there are millions of other objects, but all are objects through which Consciousness or the Source or Energy or God functions. All are instruments through which God functions. So there is no separation. Separation exists only in duality. It has to exist because it is duality, but the final understanding makes it clear that only life or the functioning of the Manifestation is in duality. What really exists prior to the duality, half a second prior to the Big Bang, is Unicity. *Consciousness is all there is.* So, that one functioning in duality, living in duality, continues to function in duality with the *total* acceptance that there is duality only so long as that body-mind organism is there. You see?

SWAMIJI (Leaning forward towards Ramesh, speaking very softly and deeply) – I *do*, actually.

RAMESH Sometimes when there is a certain amount of age and the body is rather tired, the sage is never afraid of death. Why is the sage never afraid of death at any moment? Because he has never been afraid of life. I repeat, why is the sage never afraid of death? Because he has never been afraid of life. He has been participating in life, having the pleasure and the pain and the hurt, but knowing that it is no one doing it to me. So he has been participating in life without pride, without guilt, without hatred, without envy or jealousy. So, he has been living in duality because the body-mind organism is there in duality, but with the full understanding that he is nothing but Unicity, or more accurately, *all there is, is Unicity. All there is, is Consciousness. All this is just a play in duality.*

SWAMIJI What you said just before, when you corrected yourself, you said one thing and then you corrected yourself...

RAMESH I said "more accurately".

SWAMIJI Yes, more accurately. You used a term the other day, perhaps you can just correct me if I am wrong: the only uncontestable Truth is "I AM". And then I noticed that the other Swami, his book is called I *Am That*... I am going to be a Buddhist nit-picker here and say, wouldn't it be more correct to say: "The only uncontestable Truth is that 'I am not'"?

RAMESH No – that *"me" is not*. English is the only language, Swamiji, which has a great advantage of the two words "I " and "me". The Tamil language in which Ramana Maharshi spoke didn't have it. I think most languages don't. He spoke using "I" as the "me". "Who am I?" That was his self-inquiry. But when he said: "Who am I?", "I" is the me, the ego who has to find out is there a "me" or not. So, when Ramana Maharshi used the word "I" in Tamil he meant the word "me" in English. But in Tamil there was no word for "I". So he said "I" as the "me" and "I-I-I" as the Source. He had to use the word "I" for the "me" and "I-I-I" as real "*I*". I know what you are saying is that "I am that" is not the most accurate statement. I agree entirely.

SWAMIJI Because there is no "*I*" to be there.

RAMESH Yes, because what is generally meant is the

"me". So who is told, the ego is told: "You are *That*". I have somehow intuitively never liked this. Therefore my expression has been *"That is all there is."*

SWAMIJI   I like that better!

RAMESH   *"That* is all there is." So there is truly no *you* who are to be told that *you are That*. What I am saying is that there is no you. And that is exactly what the ego comes to after this self-investigation, that   *there is, is Consciousness.*

SWAMIJI *Impersonal* Consciousness...

RAMESH   That's right, Impersonal Consciousness, the I, the Source, Unicity, the Noumenon, or God, or Energy, whatever you call it.

SWAMIJI   Well, say in Sanskrit, what would you call it? What does the *Bhagavad Gita* call it? What is the term – *Atman?*

RAMESH   Yes, *Atman*, and even there what the intellect has done is to say *Atman* is the individual personalized awareness, and *Paramatman* is the *Impersonal Awareness*. More confusion.

SWAMIJI (*Laughing*) So the Buddhists aren't the only ones! (*Lots of laughter from participants!*)

RAMESH   You see, that is why I say any scripture of any religion is a concept, liable to interpretation. Therefore, what do you have – *Advaita, Visishta Advaita* (special *Advaita*), and *Dvaita*…

SWAMIJI For the more intellectual ones!

ON ENLIGHTENMENT

How does an Enlightened being know that he is Enlightened? The question itself is an admission that the very basis of the subject has been missed: when the very basis of Self-realization is that the sense of individual volition, the sense of personal doership has been completely lost or annihilated, who can know, who would need to know? – and what would he want to know? Who is "to do the knowing" – and knowing what? Knowledge cannot be separate from the knowing of it; what else can sound be other than the hearing of it? The eye can see everything but it cannot see that which is doing the seeing. "Consciousness", being merely a conceptual symbol for that which is doing the cognizing, cannot have any objective quality that could be cognized.

What is Self-realization? The simple answer is that It can only be that which remains when this "thinking", this "conceptualizing", this trying to visualize and objectivize That which Itself does the thinking, the visualizing! In other words, the very objectivizing of what is sought – Self-realization – is the only obstacle. Thinking of that which I am seeking and the way to acquire it is the obstacle. To put it another way, the realization what-

we-are – that which is sought – cannot be "known" nor acquired, with phenomenal, conceptual effort: It can only happen. The happening needs a vacant mind, the total acceptance that trying not to make an effort is as potent a form of obstruction as making an effort. There cannot be any prescriptive method of stopping the thinking, the conceptualizing. Thinking can and must stop without any effort by the conceptual entity. It can only happen, if it is supposed to happen.

If there is nothing that the seeker can do or cannot do, the question arises: what is all the seeking about? The answer is simple: there never was a seeker; the seeking began as part of the conceptual play of phenomenality. What the conceptual seeker seeks is the end of the seeking, and the end of the seeking cannot happen without the end of the seeker; the end of the seeker can happen only when the conceptual seeker comes to the realization – Self-realization – that there never was a seeker to do any seeking, and indeed that there never was anything to be sought.

RAHASIA Is it correct to say: "I am a potential God", or "I am potential God"– is it correct? I compare it to being like I am a drop in the ocean but I don't know what the ocean is because I haven't been there. Or can I say: "I am God", which is popular with the Westerners to say "I am God already"?

RAMESH You see, the point is "I am God" means there is truly an "I" who is told he is this God. What I am saying is all there is is the Source, or God. And whatever is told that he or she is God really doesn't exist, it's a fiction created by the divine hypnosis.

RAHASIA It's the unhappy ego that wants to be Enlightened and wanted to hear that.

RAMESH Yes, and that has been beautifully put by the Buddha: "*Samsara* is *Dukkha*." But he wanted to pinpoint the *Dukkha*. Therefore he didn't say *samsara* is 5% *Sukkha* and 95% *Dukkha*. He said *Samsara is Dukkha and Nirvana is peace, Shanti*. But, he added, "*they are not two*." That is, it is not that life which is *Dukkha* is Bombay, and *Nirvana* which is peace is Paris. Then it would be simple if you had the money – you could get into a plane and leave Bombay and go to Paris! (*Laughter!*). But he said, "*Samsara is Dukkha, Nirvana is peace, but they are not two*." In other words what he said was, you have to find your *Nirvana*, peace, while living in *samsara*. You see? You have to find your *Nirvana*, peace, while living in *samsara*. And that happens only with this self-investigation. "Who is unhappy? I am unhappy." That is the me, the ego, "I am unhappy". Then, the ego is told: "Why are you unhappy?" Because something good happens, "I am proud", something bad happens, "I feel guilty, and I am told I have committed a sin." So, "I am unhappy" is basically because of the enormous awesome load of sin and guilt and added to it, hatred.

So how does the peace of *Nirvana* happen while you are living in this *samsara* of *dukkha*? If you are able to get rid of the awesome burden of sin and guilt and pride and hatred then you have the peace of *Nirvana* while being in *samsara* – while being in *samsara*, which you cannot escape, you still suffer the pains and pleasures of life. Pains and pleasures of life happen, but understanding that basically they are just happenings, you don't get involved in the pains and pleasures through pride and guilt and hatred. I repeat, pains and pleasures and hurt happen as part of life. When you are able to accept the pain, pleasure and hurt of life as part of life, without getting involved in pride and guilt and hatred, then the pains and pleasures are taken as something which happen and then go. They have been described in several instances as being like waves on the ocean. There is a gust of wind, there is a wave; there is storm, the waves are higher. And whether the gust of wind or the storm happens is not in my control. So whether the small wave happens or a huge tidal wave happens is accepted as something that happens over which I have no control. So these pleasures and pains in life continue but there is no involvement of the ego. The involvement of the ego results in pride if an action is accepted by society, sin and guilt if the society says it is a bad action, and hatred for someone if I consider someone has hurt me. But the hatred doesn't happen if I accept that the hurt happened to me, not because someone can hurt me but because it was the destiny of this body-mind organism according to the will of God to be hurt. So the hurt is also accepted.

BHISHMA I have a question. Is Enlightenment happening suddenly, or can it also happen gradually, like my Teacher was speaking about?

RAMESH You see, are you saying that the happening of

Self-realization is dependent on the age of the body? Is that your question? That is your question, isn't it? "Is Self-realization happening dependent on the age of the body?" Is that what you are saying?

BHISHMA Yes.

RAMESH Oh, no! Now Ramana Maharshi, he never had to seek, he was never a seeker, he never had the problem: "Do I go to this Teacher or that Teacher? Do I do *bhakti* or do I do *kundalini* yoga?" He never had the problem. He never was a seeker.

BHISHMA But did it happen to him spontaneously?

RAMESH Yes. Suddenly he had an experience and it was so total...

BHISHMA But it happens for some people, like what I can see for myself, the witness is growing, and ...

RAMESH But, how long it takes – but, first is, make no mistake – *who* is asking this question? The ego is asking this question about Enlightenment which he wants, the *ego* wants. Therefore the ego has to be told quite squarely, first you are talking about when the Enlightenment will happen, and I say even the happening of the Enlightenment is not in your control.

BHISHMA I know that.

RAMESH So, Enlightenment may not even happen. And if

it happens because it is the will of God; how long it takes is also the will of God. So it may happen suddenly as in the case of Ramana Maharshi, or it may take a long time.

BHISHMA Because it is always said that, for example, there are different levels of Enlightenment, like first, second and third, and the first is kind of a glimpse, and the second is the third eye opening, and then ...

RAMESH So how many stages?

BHISHMA Three.

RAMESH Someone else mentioned to me seven stages. Someone else may say twelve stages All that is conceptual, making it more complicated and telling them that it is not such an easy thing. "It is very complicated – if you come to me I'll explain it to you." You see? And I am saying it is so simple. All you have to do is be able to see it. And even that is not in your control. So you will see this simple thing only if it is God's will and the destiny, but the point is that it is simple.

BHISHMA So you mean that even if somebody declares himself Enlightened, even that is not in his control?

RAMESH That is correct. So, if someone wants to make money and he has some idea of this subject, then he will announce himself in various ways, through the supposed disciples, or whatever, that he is an Enlightened one. Therefore, when people ask me if I am able to realize when Self-realization has happened, I say that may be difficult, but I can recognize when Self-realization has not happened. (Soft laughter). Self-realization has not happened when the ego wants the whole world to know that he is Self-realized, and he is very unhappy when people don't want to accept him as Self-realized. Then it has not happened. If it has happened, what has happened? Peace has happened. So if someone wants to be known as a spiritual teacher, there is a wanting. Therefore Self-realization cannot have happened.

BHISHMA So if there is still suffering going on, it may not have happened?

RAMESH Suffering happens as part of life, I told you. Even the sage has pain, so what really suffers?

BHISHMA So suffering comes from the thinking mind?

RAMESH Psychological suffering. But physical suffering can happen to the body-mind organism of a sage if that is the destiny.

BHISHMA But he doesn't identify with it any more, so he doesn't suffer...

RAMESH You are absolutely correct, but you must make a very clear distinction about that which happens spontaneously. When someone asked my Guru in the last days of his life when he was really suffering with the pain of cancer: "Maharaj, are you in great pain?" He promptly spontaneously answered: " Yes, there is great pain".

BHISHMA So he was not suffering anymore?

RAMESH The suffering was there, suffering was there, but the real point was not "Is he suffering?" but "What was suffering?"

BHISHMA So the body-mind organism is suffering.

RAMESH That is correct. Therefore the body-mind organism that is suffering may utter a moan or say something. like Christ saying: "Father, why has thou forsaken me?" Or Ramakrishna talking to the Divine Mother Kali: "Mother, why are you making me suffer so much?" That is the identification with the body-mind organism. That identification is crying out in pain, you see? So the crying out in pain is not the sage crying out, but the body-mind organism is crying out. What is the sage doing? The sage, that is mere identification without any sense of personal doership, that weak ego is merely witnessing the pain and the pain taking the action of the shouting or the moaning. So what I am saying is this, if the suffering of the body-mind organism or the shouting or the moaning had happened through some other body-mind organism, what would the sage have done? He would have witnessed it. At the most, if it were someone else, he might have felt sympathy. So, if the body-mind organism of a sage is suffering from pain, then the suffering of the pain will be witnessed by the sage as if it is the suffering in any body-mind organism. As far as the suffering is concerned, the sage does not make a difference between his body and some other body. If Ramakrishna had seen someone else suffering, he might have cried out: "Mother why are you making him suffer so?" Now he said: " Why are you making me suffer?"

BHISHMA Is the witness also coming from the weak part of the mind?

RAMESH The witnessing is the impersonal witnessing. The Self-realization or Enlightenment in action is witnessing. I repeat, Enlightenment or Self-realization in action is witnessing.

BHISHMA What is the difference between witnessing and Consciousness?

RAMESH The difference is between *impersonal* witnessing and *personal* observing. Again, a conceptual separation of words, but in order to understand you have to use the words. So my concept is that the difference is impersonal witnessing, different from personal observing. In what way is it different? Personal observing is innately judging something as good or bad. In impersonal witnessing, everything is merely witnessed.

UNDENIABLE TRUTH

The Source is the unperceivable Reality; the manifestation is the perceivable appearance, the illusion. We are truly not concerned with the Source in any intellectual seeking except to understand it as that from which every "thing" has emanated. Therefore, to describe – to attempt to describe – that which cannot be perceived and therefore described, is sheer foolishness. It is the cause of much unnecessary confusion, frustration and controversy in one's spiritual search.

The Hindu concept of the Source is given in the Mundaka Upanishad as: "In the highest golden sheath is Brahman, stainless, without parts; Pure it is, the light of lights. This is what the knowers of the Self know. The sun shines not there, nor the moon and stars; there lightnings shine not; where then could this fire be? His shining illumines all this world. Brahman, verily, is this Deathless."

The Buddha has described the Source as Emptiness. Says the Udana: Where water, earth, heat and wind find no footing, there no stars gleam, no sun is made visible, there shines no moon, there the darkness is not found; when the sage, the brahmin, himself in wisdom knows this place, he is freed from the form and formless realms, from happiness and suffering."

As Ramana Maharshi has said, all that a spiritual seeker has to find out is: " Who am I?" – Who or what is this "me" who seeks he does not know what? Basically, this "me", the spiritual seeker is one species of object, which together with thousands of species of objects on land, air and water, constitutes the totality of Manifestation extended in space-time. This is all that is to be deeply understood, that an object cannot seek anything, and therefore, the apparent seeker, with all his misery, is nothing but an illusion that is part of the total illusion – Maya – that the entire Manifestation is. If this deep realization happens – no object can achieve it – then there is freedom: freedom from the spiritual seeking.

BHISHMA It seems to be that the only undeniable Truth is that something exists. Or, there is a Source. But it is very different from saying I AM, I EXIST.

RAMESH For the Source, Consciousness-at-rest, there is no question of awareness. But when the Source, or Consciousness, activizes itself in the Manifestation, the Consciousness becomes aware of itself. That is the impersonal awareness, I AM.

BHISHMA But this is a hypothesis.

RAMESH Of course it is.

BHISHMA There is no way for me to know that.

RAMESH Oh yes, you know "I AM". It simply means "you exist". Can you deny that? I AM – can anyone deny that?

BHISHMA Well, supposing I was a computer...

RAMESH Supposing you are you...

BHISHMA If I am a computer, the software could say "There is a computer, it exists", but the "I" part seeing this is just invisible software.

RAMESH All I am saying is, is there not an awareness that you are, that you exist? Can any human being deny that? No human being can deny that he or she exists, which is I AM.

BHISHMA Right.

RAMESH And that awareness is not that "I am Ramesh", not that "I exist as Ramesh", but I EXIST, whatever the name, whatever the body-mind organism; therefore it is an impersonal awareness. But, you are quite right. The moment I talk about it, it becomes a concept. But the impersonal awareness is there in every body-mind organism. The moment we talk about it, it becomes a concept. Even if we don't talk about it, the feeling is always there, in the waking state.

BISHMA It still seems to me that it could still be that the feeling "I AM" is a complete illusion that disappears at death.

RAMESH It is, it is. That's what the Advaita says. The only Reality is Consciousness-at-rest, the Source. So what has emerged from the Source is only an appearance, and an appearance is an illusion, you see? An appearance is an illusion, which after the energy of the Big Bang has exhausted itself, it goes back into the potential.

BHISHMA Space and time are also created at the moment of the Big Bang.

RAMESH Exactly! Yes.

BHISHMA So it is absurd to try to talk about the moments before the Big Bang because time did not exist.

RAMESH That's the point. The human being can only talk

about something after the Big Bang. And what is before the Big Bang no human being can ever know. That is correct.

BHISHMA There still seems to be an arbitrary jump that you are making between "the Source exists" and that "I am a part of that Source", or that Awareness.

RAMESH It is a concept. That is what I have always said, it is a concept. Whatever I am talking about is a concept, whatever any sage has ever said is a concept. Whatever any scripture of any religion has ever said is a concept, a concept being a creation of the mind.

VISITOR In a way, for a sage, for you it is not a concept, it is an experience because you did the jump already.

RAMESH I'm sorry...?

VISITOR You did the jump already. So, for you its true, its not a concept any more.

RAMESH No, what I am saying is that for the ego who has investigated it from personal experience, the concept becomes the truth, but the truth that the ego arrives at is part of the functioning of the Manifestation. And if the Manifestation is seen as an illusion, the functioning of the Manifestation is also an illusion. So, that everything is an illusion is the basis. Therefore, as Ramana Maharshi said: "There is no creation, there is no dissolution." This is the final Truth. "There is no creation, there is no dissolution."

VISITOR Then it is not explainable in words any more.

RAMESH That is the explanation. We think it is creation, we think it will be dissolved at the end of the energy of the Big Bang; it is just a concept, it is just an illusion.

VISITOR So there is no way to become convinced of it, it has to be found?

RAMESH Who has to be convinced of it? A computer. How can a computer be convinced, and convinced of what? Nothing has happened. And that really is what happens in the case of sage. He accepts life as it happens as a movie. The sage suffers with those who are suffering.

So he's not uninvolved in the movie. He participates in the movie. If there is humor, he laughs, if there is suffering, tears may arise in his eyes, and if it is a horror film, fear may arise, but with all this participating in the movie, the basic understanding is that the movie is an appearance which could not be there in the absence of the Reality of the screen. Life is a movie that could not happen in the absence of the Reality of the screen of Consciousness. That the sage is always aware of. The sage is always aware of the Reality of the screen, while participating in the movie.

DOES FREE WILL EXIST?

According to almost every sage, our conceptual bondage lies in the fact that we "prefer" certain things because they are agreeable, and "reject" certain others as being not agreeable. Perhaps they expect us to go deeper into these words. The preference and rejection imply the exercise of volition in choice by a supposed autonomous "entity". The question, therefore, is does such an entity with self-nature exist? If not, there has been an erroneous identification with the supposed entity. It is, therefore, only dis-identification with the non-existing entity that will suspend the exercise of the conceptual volition which is the cause of the bondage. What would remain, then, is only an identification, without volition, to enable the body-mind organism to function according to the will of God (or according to the Cosmic Law): "The remnants of a burnt rope", as Ramana Maharshi put it.

This is the whole story: nothing to be achieved, only one thing to be given up – the false sense of personal doership.

ANNYA What if you don't know what is the right thing to do in life?

RAMESH It is a good question. The body-mind organism called Annya is so programmed that she would always like to do the right thing, but she doesn't always know what the right thing is. Is that the problem?

ANNYA Yes.

RAMESH Annya says: "I like to do the right thing, but I don't know what is right under the circumstances. I would like to do God's will." But, Annya doesn't know God's will. That is the problem, isn't it? Annya would like to do what God wants, but the problem is that Annya does not know what is God's will. You see, what happens is that Annya doesn't know, but God does! And God will make you do exactly what he wants you to do.

ANNYA So in times of not knowing you are just with not knowing?

RAMESH No, at times of not knowing you make a decision. Now, even making that decision may be easy for some and not so easy for others. Some people may search for a solution. Or some people may even flip a coin. So whichever way you decide, just decide what you want to do with the understanding that whatever you have decided to do will not happen unless it is God's will.

ANNYA So there's no more worry about it!

RAMESH That's the point, that's exactly the point. Do whatever you want to do, knowing that if it happens it could not have happened unless it is the will of God. But, Annya, don't forget, if an action has happened because it is God's will, then the consequences should not hurt Annya – that is not so! That is important to remember. An action happens because it is God's will and the consequences happen also because it is God's will. And, the consequences may affect not only Annya, but a number of others. You see? An action happens because it is God's will. And, the consequences affect whomever they are supposed to affect. Therefore you need not worry about it.

SWAMIJI I just wanted to comment – that was the most complicated way of saying what somebody else would say as: "Do what you think is right, and don't worry about the consequences if your intentions were right."

RAMESH And why? I have explained to you why. This takes away all the tension.

SWAMIJI Yes, it's quite clear. Uninhibited free action.

RAMESH Exactly, therefore the question arises, Swamiji: "Do I have free will?" So I say investigate that free will and you will find that the apparent free will is counterfeit. If you try to find out what that free will is, free will is doing what I want to do. What is free will? Being able to do what I want to do. And what I want to do is what I am programmed to do, and what I like to do is what I am programmed to like. So you have free will. But that free will is based on something over which you have no control. That's why I call it "counterfeit".

VISITOR (*Sounding a bit angry...*) What about someone like Hitler or Stalin or whomever, name them, there are thousands of guys like that. They are absolutely okay then? What they are doing... they are just following their free will?

RAMESH No, no. *They* don't exist. Only body-mind organisms exist, which have been programmed to do exactly what they have done, and whatever you think they have done could not have happened unless it was God's will. Let me put it this way. Until a year or two ago, there was a body-mind organism called Mother Teresa, so programmed that only what society calls good deeds happened. At the same time, there were several body-mind organisms that were so programmed that only bad actions, evil actions happened, and the society called them psychopaths. So, my point is a body-mind organism of a psychopath and the programming therein and the body-mind organism of a Mother Teresa with the appropriate programming therein were both created by the same Source, by the same Energy, by the same God – that is all I am saying – so that such actions could happen together with the relevant consequences.

VISITOR (*With frustration...*) Where does responsibility come into the game? Do we just let them kill some more millions and don't worry about it, or do we interfere?

RAMESH Do whatever you like! You forget what I just said. Do whatever you like. So if you want to interfere, then interfere! That is why it is so important to be clear that this understanding doesn't prevent you from doing whatever you think you like, or whatever you think you should do.

VISITOR What about when we come to the point where we have two opposite opinions? One says: "Don't interfere, this is my inner business", and the other says: "This is no more your inner business, you have crossed the borders and I have to stop you." Then you have something like two bulls or buffalos standing head-to-head facing each other, and where is the measurement of when it is right to stop something and where is the measurement that says you can go on?

Ramesh So your question is again the same thing: you would like to do what is right, and you would not like to do what is wrong.

Visitor (*More frustrated than ever!*) So now anyone can just say: "I am following God's will." Perhaps the European government says: "We are following God's will." So who is following God's will?

Ramesh Both! And that is why we have the friction! The friction *had* to happen! That is why the two bulls were created! Why are the fighting bulls created? Why are the fighting cocks created? So that the game of cockfighting will go on and so that the game of bullfighting will go on as part of life. Ah – you could say that this bullfighting is bad, so you can do whatever you like to stop bullfighting in Spain – and see how far you go! (*Lots of laughter!*) So, the basic I come to again and again and again, this teaching does not prevent anyone from doing exactly what he or she thinks he or she should do. What more freedom can you have? The action is God's will; the consequences are God's will. But what often actually happens is that you do not do anything that you think you should do. You say: "Someone should do something about it"!

UNBROKEN WHOLE

The Guru does not talk to individuals. He is Consciousness talking about Consciousness to Consciousness.

QUESTION The Impersonal Awareness of Being is God?

RAMESH Yes, you could say that. Or, the I AM is the Awareness of Presence. Not as any one, but the *Impersonal Awareness of Being, I AM.* That is the phenomenal presence of the Noumenal absence. The Source as a Source is not aware of itself. Potential Energy is not aware of itself as Potential Energy until it activizes itself. You see?

QUESTION So I felt one time that I recognized that I cannot be aware of the Awareness?

RAMESH That's right. Because there is no need to, you are, that's all. But when the question arises, "Who Am I?", the Impersonal Awareness has split itself into subject-object. The Impersonal Awareness, I AM, exists even in deep sleep, and that is why deep sleep is not the Source. As the Source, the Consciousness does not need to be aware of itself. Awareness of itself is only in phenomenality.

QUESTION This condition happens after death?

RAMESH After the Potential Energy has activized itself, Consciousness-at-rest has become Consciousness-in-movement and the Manifestation happens. The Consciousness which was not aware of itself in its Potential state, in its Noumenal state, becomes aware of itself in phenomenality. But in phenomenality, that I AM as an impersonal witness divides itself into subject-object, in duality.

QUESTION Because in …?

RAMESH You see, the moment the question arises, some *one* wants to know what he is, he thinks he is something else. Therefore he says I want to know what I am and then there is a split between subject-object. Then subject "he" wants to know what he is, something else. The understanding happens that whatever has happened in phenomenality that makes him ask this question, "Who am I?", or whatever, is really part of something which doesn't exist. The child of a barren woman. It just doesn't exist. It cannot exist! So the human being who wants to know what he is, or anything else, is merely something which happens in imagination. You see? So there is truly no *one* to ask any question. When that understanding becomes total, that there is truly no one to do anything, there is no one to find anything, because there is nothing to be found, then the duality gets healed into the Noumenal Awareness of just Presence – Impersonal Presence.

QUESTION But the duality is also there?

RAMESH Duality is only in phenomenality. But the understanding is that it is the same Source or Energy which functions through every object, so therefore there is no *one* doing anything, there is no *one* to experience anything, that the doing and experiencing as such is the Impersonal Awareness.

QUESTION The experiencing is the Awareness? It's just a happening in the Awareness?

RAMESH   That's right, therefore there is no one to experience anything. There is no one to experience happiness, there is no one to experience pain. Pain and happiness both are an experiencing, which is itself the Impersonal Awareness. The Impersonal Awareness is the experiencing in pheomenality, which even that phenomenality truly doesn't exist. You see? And that can only happen. Why can it only happen? Because a phenomenal object – who wants to know – basically is an object and an object cannot know anything. So the object wanting to know something – what has happened? The object with an independent existence of its own due to *maya* or divine hypnosis, considers itself the subject and wants to know something, whatever it is, wants to know something, or get something, so an object creates a subject-object relationship. And how does it do it? It can only do it this way: an object usurps the subjectivity of the Pure Subject, the Source – the Source is the only Subject – and an object which has a given name, it wants to know something. Therefore what that named object has done is to become the subject. So in order to become the subject, one has usurped the subjectivity of the pure Subject and turned the Subjectivity, the Source, into an object, which this object wants to know. You see? This, I am tempted to say is the original sin, if there ever is a sin! You see what I mean? It means an object, considering itself the Subject, wanting to know the Subject and thereby turning the Subject into an object! Some *one* wanting to know what he is, someone wanting to know the Source, means he is the subject and he has turned his real nature, or whatever you call it, the Source, into an object, which is impossible; that's why the suffering! You see? So, then, by the grace of God, or because it is the destiny of a body-mind organism, the sudden understanding happens: "How can an object ever know the Source?" When there is the realization of the impossibility of an object ever knowing the Subject, then the whole thing collapses, and the individual wanting to know the subject collapses into the Impersonal Presence, and in the Impersonal Presence there is no one wanting to know anything, you see. So the final understanding is, *an object cannot know anything.* So all the questions then collapse. How can an object have any questions to find out an answer? An object is an object. So the final realization is that every human being is an object through which the Source functions, and it is the same Source, the same Consciousness functioning through every body-mind organism.

QUESTION   When this Consciousness-at-rest goes into movement, am I the Consciousness which identifies itself with this body-mind organism?

RAMESH Yes! Correct! And, on top of it, that Consciousness makes this object, by divine hypnosis, think it is the Subject, as part of the functioning of life. And therefore I say, when the Source created the ego with a sense of personal doership, it also started the process of destroying the ego in a limited number of cases. And in those limited number of cases, those body-mind organisms were so programmed that this kind of thinking, this kind of investigating happens. So the seeking of what really exists happens because a body-mind organism is so programmed that the seeking had to happen. You don't have to worry about the seeking, because the One who started the seeking will take the seeking on its natural course. You don't need to worry about it!

QUESTION When Ramana Maharshi says you should not identify with the body, does it mean in the sense of identifying with actions of the body with the sense of personal doership – not identifying with thinking of actions as you are the doer?

RAMESH Yes. So basically what he says is this: whatever has happened is happening as something perceived. It is a perception. And you are an object, so the perception happens; an object cannot perceive anything, an object cannot perceive itself or any other object. Coming right down to it, *one* cannot perceive! "Perceive" means perceiving through any sense, seeing, hearing, tasting, touching, smelling. Whatever "happens" is the word perceive. So what he means is that there is no *one* individual to perceive; an individual is only an object and an object cannot perceive anything. So any perceiving that is done is not by any *one* doing any perceiving, because the one who thinks he is perceiving is an object, and yet the perceiving happens. Therefore, the perceiving happens, and that perceiving that happens is the Noumenon perceiving, or the Source perceiving, and there is no individual to do anything. So the perceiving that happens is part of the functioning of the Source in its Manifestation. The Potential Energy has activized itself and the Potential Energy is doing the perceiving through the various objects programmed for the perceiving to happen.

QUESTION So the perceiving happens in the Source?

RAMESH No, Noumenon does the perceiving in phenomenality.

QUESTION What do you mean "does"? Isn't the perceiving just an appearance?

RAMESH That's right – the perceiving happens in Consciousness by the Consciousness. The perceiving by Consciousness is part of the movement in Consciousness. So, *all there is, is Consciousness*, whether at rest, or in action. The basic point is that it is Consciousness objectivizing itself in movement, and part of that movement is Consciousness doing the perceiving, doing the action of perceiving the action. The final truth is that *nothing has really happened, nothing is happening, nothing will happen*, it is an illusion. That is what it really comes down to!

~

*All that is necessary is to understand the physics of
God: His Indivisible Nature - the Unbroken Whole.
This understanding makes every universe and atom
confess: "I am just a helpless puppet that cannot dance
without the movement of His Hand."*

(With apologies to Hafiz, the "all-knowing".)
— RAMESH BALSEKAR

Conclusion

∿

Shen Hui, the Zen Master declared: "There is a difference between Awakening and Deliverance: the former is sudden, thereafter deliverance is gradual… In fact, what we mean by 'sudden Enlightenment' is the perfect equivalence of phenomenal understanding with universal principle: this is not reached by any stages at all."

Wei Wu Wei gives an explanation: "The sudden coincidence of relative comprehension with absolute apprehension, whereby the division of mind into subject and object is healed so that its wholeness supervenes, in a spontaneous absence of duration, throws open the way to deliverance from 'bondage' to our conceptual universe."

What is the "bondage to our conceptual universe"? It is the sense of personal doership, the basis of interhuman relationships: friendship and enmity, love and hatred. It is the separation of "me" as the doer of "my" actions, and "you" as the doer of "your" actions – you are either my friend or my enemy, depending upon how your actions affect me. This is the "division of mind into subject and object." This division or separation between subject and object can be healed only when there is a total, absolute acceptance, based on personal experience, that, to use the Buddha's words: "Events happen, deeds are done, but there is no individual doer thereof."

Thus the "bondage to our conceptual universe" is the interhuman relationship based upon the separation between subject and object, which itself is based on the sense of personal doership. When this sense of personal doership is removed with the apperception that all action is a happening (according to God's Will or the Cosmic Law) and not something done by anyone, this bondage disappears. This bondage is experienced as suffering caused by the monstrous load on the mind, the load of pride and arrogance, guilt and shame for actions which we think we are doing, together with the load of hatred and enmity, jealousy and envy for actions which we think others are doing.

The result of this healing between the subject and object, between the "me" and the "you" is that *there is an immediate acceptance of whatever is in the moment*, without judging any action without attaching any blame (or credit) to any "one" for any action. Nothing then seems really to "matter": there is no "one" to whom anything can matter. Life becomes an entertainment; some event brings tears to the eyes, some event brings a smile or a laugh.

What *then* is life like?

a) You are watching the big tennis match on the television. The champion is getting a beating, the match is almost over, and then, suddenly, inexplicably, something happens: the champion comes back forcefully from behind, there is nothing he can do wrong, and he wins the match and the tournament. Great entertainment!

b) The millionaire businessman takes a big gamble. There is a big miscalculation and the millions have suddenly evaporated. Worse still, all those years, too much money has spoilt the children beyond redemption and they are now in a helpless condition. Great entertainment, no matter who is concerned: me, you or him. No one has any control over life, a dream, a movie!

c) The wife of 60 years of marriage is seriously ill in a hospital. An operation is necessary, and the chances of recovery are not good. The children assure the old man that they will not let him stay alone. The old man smiles – he does not have many years to live, the future will be another experience. During the operation, the kidneys, for no apparent reason, fail. The surgeon discusses the situation with the son and it is decided that the patient, in that state of health will not be put on dialysis – it would be living death. By the time the surgeon comes back to the surgery, the kidneys have, suddenly, inexplicably, snapped back into action. The operation is successful – a miracle. Great entertainment!

d) The sage is dying, but there is a gentle smile on his face. He opens his eyes and sees people crying. He asks why, and he is told that they do not want to lose him. The sage smiles broadly and says: "Where can I go? I can only BE where I have always been: here, there, everywhere – and nowhere!"

The   final joke in the conceptual universe: after "awakening", who is there to be concerned with "deliverance"?! To be so concerned would still be bondage to the conceptual universe.

~

EPILOGUE

~

HAPPINESS AND SUFFERING

What the Buddha found when he was "Awake" during that special night under the Bodhi tree could be interpreted as his being awake to the fact that what he was looking for was not the happiness as compared or contrasted with suffering, but that which transcended both suffering and happiness. What is experienced as suffering and happiness is merely a positive or negative experience for the conceptual individual. When this volitional individuality was lost for the Buddha, he was awake to the fact that neither happiness nor suffering existed for him any longer. What remained for him was termed as *Ananda* or *Sat-Chit-Ananda*, which has been translated in English as "bliss".

In his *Amritanubhava*, a classic in the Marathi language, the sage Jnaneshwar explains the significance of the three oft-repeated attributes of the Absolute in Hindu philosophy. "*Sat*" (being), "*Chit*" (Consciousness) and "*Ananda*" (bliss) are the three attributes of the Brahman as described by the Vedas, but they are not to be considered separately because even in their entirety they cannot affect the Brahman, just as the poisonous nature of poison does not affect the poison itself. The "beingness" and "consciousness" finally end in the ultimate *BLISS*; indeed, since there is no one to experience the ultimate "bliss", the beingness and the consciousness cannot exist independently in the absolute state, where there can be no conditions perceptible to the senses. Jnaneshwar further explains that the "bliss" in the absolute state – transcending as it does the experiencer, the experienced bliss and the experiencing – annihilates the other two aspects. Jnaneshwar seems to imply that relatively speaking, the expression "*Sat-Chit-Ananda*" could be conceptualized that on the "*Sat*", the Consciousness-at-rest, spontaneously arises the "*Chit*" – the movement (*I AM*) together with the manifested universe – and the realization of the basic identity of the unmanifest and the unmanifested universe results in *BLISS*. The realization that phenomenality is merely the objectivization of noumenality, and not a separate thing, breaks the separation or the duality between "me" and the "other" and thereby results in *BLISS*. "When all conceptualizing ceases, what is left?", asks Jnaneshwar. What is left is apparently "nothing" phenomenally, but, noumenally, it is absolute presence, the potential plenum, the *BLISS*.

The word "*Ananda*" has always been translated as "bliss". Any word would be a concept, but perhaps "peace" would be more appropriate inasmuch as it would not raise any expectations that the word "bliss" could raise for the conceptual individual entity.

STAGES OF UNDERSTANDING*

The Buddhists have an excellent summary of not just how the enlightened see the world, but how the enlightened happened to come to see the way they do. The summary involves three stages of understanding. The first degree of understanding is the seeing by the involved individual. The second degree is when there is a certain amount of understanding. Finally, there is total understanding.

* *"Stages of Understanding": From Ramesh S. Balsekar, Consciousness Speaks, Advaita Press, Redondo Beach, California 1992, and Zen Publications, Mumbai, 1996, p. 220.*

First, mountains and rivers are seen as mountains and rivers. An individual identified subject is seeing an object. This is total involvement. This is what the ordinary person does.

Second, mountains and rivers are no longer seen as mountains and rivers. Obejcts are seen as the mirrored objectivization of the subject. They are perceived as illusory objects in Consciousness and therefore unreal.

Finally, mountains and rivers are once more seen as mountains and rivers. That is, on being awakened, they are known as Consciousness itself, manifesting as mountains and rivers. Subject and objects are not seen as being separate.

In this summary, mountains and rivers refer to the world at large, including the totality of the human population.

The involved individual will first see objects as an individual subject seeing objects. He considers himself a separate entity seeing other objects. Seeing other objects or events creates reactions in him as an individual. So, the individual organism reacts to what is seen.

In the second stage, when there is understanding that all of this is a dream and unreal, the view changes and he begins to see that no event really matters. He sees them as unreal because, as the subject, he transcends the appearance. Appearance is something that comes about in Consciousness. When understanding arises at this level, there is so much enjoyment of the understanding that the individual concerned often has great difficulty keeping it to himself. He goes about telling the world: "All of this is unreal!" In trying to tell others that the world is unreal, he wants to change the world, change the perceptions of others. He doesn't realize that the change has to come from within. And so, wanting to change the world, he goes about creating problems for himself. These problems which the second stage brings about settle down only in the third stage.

In the third stage, objects are seen not by an individual, nor by an object seeing an object, nor a subject seeing an object. The true perceiver is realized as that which created the appearance and that which cognizes the appearance. They are both the same. At this stage, the ultimate realization is not only that the world is unreal, but that at the same time the world is real! The world is unreal in the sense that it is dependent on Consciousness for its existence. It has no independent existence of its own. The world owes its existence to being cognized in Consciousness. If every human being and every animal suddenly became unconscious, who's to say that there is a world? The world not only wouldn't appear, but wouldn't exist.

~

Satsang, Guru Purnima, July 16, 2000

*"The Totality of Manifestation is an appearance
in Consciousness, like a dream. Its functioning
is an impersonal and self-generated process in
phenomenality: and the billions of sentient beings are
merely instruments (dreamed characters without any
kind of volition) through which this impersonal process
takes place. The clear apperception of this Truth means
the irrelevance of the individual human being as a
seeker, and therefore Enlightenment."*

∽

"*The illusory individual, along with the rest of the phenomenal manifestation, disappears into its Source as soon as its involvement in the process of conceptualizaton ceases.*"

"Self-realization is the total realization that there is no one to realize (or achieve) anything."

RAMESH S. BALSEKAR
BIOGRAPHICAL NOTES

~

Ramesh and the Teachings are inseparable. There's a body-mind organism known as Ramesh, and even in its appearance the instrument through which the words come is the Teachings. The total understanding that *No One Does Anything* happened in 1979. Ramesh had a Guru for 20 years prior, but shortly after his retirement he met his final Guru, Nisargadatta Maharaj, for whom he translated daily talks in Mumbai until Maharaj died in 1981. For most of his life Ramesh has also been devoted to Ramana Maharshi.

Ramesh is known around the world as a Master of pure Advaita, even though as a Hindu Brahmin child he was brought up surrounded by traditional Hindu spiritual practices. Being somewhat resistant, around the age of twelve years he conceded to his mother a promise of a minimal daily practice of chanting the *Ramaraksha Stotra*, which has been happening ever since. Why does he continue this practice?: he sees no reason for stopping it! The Teachings, in fact, begin with *bhakti*: what is there more devotional than "Thy Will Be Done"? And the Teachings end in *jnana*, "All there is is Consciousness": the pure knowledge of Advaita.

Ramesh might be considered a "householder" Guru –
he has lived a full and rich life, which is reflected in his
teaching. Upon meeting Ramesh, it doesn't take long to
see that he is no ordinary individual, though at first glance
that may be the impression. Prior to teaching, Ramesh
served the Bank of India for 37 years until a mandatory
retirement at age 60 in 1977. He served as the General
Manager, or President of the bank, for ten years. When
asked about his life, the answer consistently reflects the
impact of his life-long intuitive understanding that nothing
happens unless it is God's will. For example, with great
humor Ramesh explains that there was never any concern
about his promotions from the time his career began as a
bank clerk – "no boot-licking" – knowing that whatever
would happen would be according to God's will, and that
"no power on earth could prevent the promotions from
happening."

Though undoubtedly his career was brilliant, Ramesh
claims that in most of his life's pursuits, he was very
successful but not number one. It was his position as
President rather than Chairman of the Board of Directors
towards the end of his career that allowed Ramesh time
in his schedule to visit Maharaj every morning. Both
during his general education and at the London School
of Economics his class ranking was usually third, and
occasionally fourth or fifth. And for years Ramesh was
enthusiastic about golf, and though an avid player he was
rarely the top man on the team. While his golf handicap
improved considerably over the years playing only on
weekends, his strokes over par remained in the two-
digit category, never dropping into the single-digit range.

Similarly, he enjoyed badminton but was not a champion on the court. Also, there are several photos dated around sixty years ago that reveal his success as a body builder. When a surprised visitor inquires about those photographs, Ramesh admits that occasionally the photos occupied prime spots in the sports magazines, but that the acclaim was just for the category of small-statured athletes. The most highly esteemed heroes of the iron-pumping world were the massive heavy-weight giants. In reflecting on the achievements as they happened during his active life, with a twinkle in his eye Ramesh commented that God must have thought: "This is enough for you; more than that and you'll be proud." And then gently he remarked: "God has been exceedingly kind to me – there never was opportunity for pride and arrogance." Truly, there never is any pretense and always an admirable and irrefutable glow of humility and love.

This year Ramesh and Sharda celebrated sixty years of marriage, during which they raised three children. The eldest son, Ajit, died in 1990 at age 49 after long history of health problems. Their daughter Jaya lives in Bangalore where she runs a successful dairy business and her husband manages an 80 acre farm. The youngest, Shivdas, is married and lives in Mumbai where he was a top executive in a pharmaceutical company for twenty years, and is now a consultant in managerial efficiency. Ramesh is said to be a favorite uncle and grandfather.

The role as a Teacher began for Ramesh not because he wanted to be a Teacher, but by full authorization from Nisargadatta Maharaj. The command to "talk" was given once by his Guru during a talk and again shortly before his death in a loud and clear voice which came out of his body which was dying from cancer. The conversations originated in 1982, beginning with a talk with an Australian man who showed up at Ramesh's home early one morning, having travelled for nearly three hours from an ashram outside of Bombay. Sharda graciously offered him breakfast, and they talked for over an hour. The very next day the same man came again with a few others, who returned again and again, each time bringing with them a few more friends. Curiously, that was the last time Ramesh heard from this man, but so the morning talks commenced. Since that time, Ramesh has offered a number of seminars in the United States and in Europe, and he continues to speak every morning in Mumbai. When asked about attendance at the daily talks Ramesh invariably replies: "No one is invited, and everyone is welcome."

The Teachings that come through Ramesh are pure Advaita – *Consciousness is all there is*, there is only the Unbroken Whole. He closes the gap between Eastern and Western thinking. The Teachings are simple and clear and, along with the fact that Ramesh is no ordinary Indian Guru, this is perhaps why most of the people who come to him are Westerners. Even during the days as a translator for Maharaj, the combination of his Western education and cultural influence contributed to Ramesh's reputation as being the interpreter most preferred by Western visitors. The impact of the Teachings is fuelled with the force of his Total Understanding. From his own life experience Ramesh makes the Teachings for here and now. In reference to the morning talks, Ramesh himself admits with a laugh that for those with interest in the subject it's the best entertainment in Mumbai!

∼

Words, being merely the product of temporal conceptualization, have only the most limited usefulness. They can point to or describe a mango, but they can neither yield its flavor nor alleviate anyone's hunger.

– RAMESH BALSEKAR

GLOSSARY OF CONCEPTS*

∾

*The created object cannot
possibly know the Creator Subjectivity.*

abhanga

Spontaneous outpouring of a keen devotee revealing the very core of Advaita; for centuries *abhangas* have served as succinct and direct pointers to Consciousness; often put to music and sung as a bhajan; *see* Advaita, bhajan

Adi Shankara

see Shankara

Advaita

Nonduality, a + *dvaita*, not dual; all there is is Consciousness, and all phenomenal existence is illusion, *maya*; the most important branch of Vedanta philosophy; *see* Consciousness, maya, Vedanta

ahankara

Ego; *see* ego

Ananda

Peace; *see* Sat-Chit-Ananda

arises, arising

see happens, happening

Aum

The sound of these three letters, now generally considered

* Ramesh S. Balsekar, *Who Cares?!* Zen Publications, Bombay, 1999, Glossary of Concepts, p. 177.

a word, denotes Consciousness, Brahman; believed to be the most sacred mantra; the letter A stands for the world of the senses, the letter U stands for the subconscious mind, and M stands for *Prajna*, the state beyond mind; usually written as "Om"; *see* mantra

avatar

Incarnation; descent of a deity (i.e., Vishnu descending as Rama and Krishna)

awakening

see enlightenment

Bhagavad Gita

Literally the song of God; part of the *Mahabharata* in which a dialogue takes place between Lord Krishna and the warrior Arjuna just prior to the decisive battle

bhajan

Devotional practice, prayer; generally used to mean devotional words set to music and sung as a form of worship

bhakta

Devotee; often used to refer to a seeker following the path of bhakti, as distinguished from that of jnana, however, bhakti and jnana are not two; *see* jnana, seeker

bhakti

Devotion and surrendering as a path to enlightenment, however, bhakti and jnana are not two; see enlightenment, bhakta, seeking

bhoga, (bhogi)

Experience(er) of sensual reactions

body-mind organism

Mechanism through which life and living happen; part of the totality of manifestation of Consciousness in which the ego ignorantly assumes the role of apparent doership and hence separateness; the body-mind organism, not the ego, has a destiny; *see* destiny, ego, manifestation

Brahma

One of the gods of the Hindu trinity, *see* trinity

brahmachari (m), brahmacharini (f)

One who leads the life of *brahmacharya*

brahmacharya

Living in Brahman; enquiry into Brahman, or Consciousness; traditionally, although mistakenly, it has come to mean celibacy

Brahman

Consciousness, Source, Totality, the Absolute; a concept for the ultimate Reality in Hinduism; see Consciousness

brain

In the body-mind organism the mechanism which spontaneously *reacts* according to its programming, without *judging* the thoughts received or the input of the senses; *see* body-mind organism, programming, thinking mind, thought, working mind

Chit

Consciousness; *see Sat-Chit-Ananda*

concept

Anything that can be agreed with or disagreed with; any thought, idea, experience, name, thing, entity, or no-thing

conditioning

All the experiences of a body-mind organism—over which it has no control—of its entire environment (parents, family, society, culture, geography, school, etc.) which form the patterns and responses of the brain; *see* body-mind organism, brain, ego, programming

Consciousness

All there is is Consciousness; the basic perennial principle behind all religions and spiritual paths before corruption by interpretations and formal rituals; It has no aspects or qualities; It *cannot* be conceptualised but is given a name so It can be indicated or pointed to; It is *referred* to by many names—God, I-I, Noumenon, Potential, Reality, Self, Source, Subjectivity, Tao, That, Totality, Truth, Unicity, etc.; unmanifested It is referred to as being "at rest" or transcendent, manifested It is referred to as being "in action" or immanent; Consciousness not aware of Itself becomes aware of Itself as I Am; *see* concept, I Am

consciousness

All there is is Consciousness, but lower-case c indicates Consciousness identified with a body-mind organism; *see* Consciousness-in-action, ego, I Am

Consciousness-at-rest

Consciousness unmanifested, transcendent;

Potential unpotentialized; *see* Consciousness
Consciousness-in-action

Consciousness manifest, immanent; Consciousness reflected within Itself as the totality of manifestation; *see* Consciousness

darshan

Seeing, meeting

death

Death is only of the body-mind organism and ego, the sense of a separate and personal identity; at death the energies of Consciousness-in-action which had assumed personal identity in life as a body-mind organism return to the pool of Consciousness; *see* ego, body-mind organism, pool of Consciousness

deep sleep

The state in which the I Am is present without any aspect of manifestation, which also means no personal or ego identity; temporary death; *see* ego, I Am

destiny

All there is is Consciousness; there is no doer and no free will—all is the impersonal functioning of Consciousness, or God's will; life is a movie which is produced, written, cast, directed, acted, and watched by Consciousness on the screen of Consciousness; the body-mind organism has a destiny, the ego has no destiny; the key, which is not in the control of the *apparent* individual, is the complete acceptance of What-Is; decisions have to be made, so live life *as if* there is free will, making decisions with your standards of ethics, morality, and responsibility, and whatever the decision is will be God's will; *see* Consciousness, What-Is

dharma

The programming of the body-mind organism; inherent property; natural characteristic; in Hinduism the firm code of conduct and duty of the individual; *see* body-mind organism, programming

dhyana

Meditation; *see* meditation

Divine hypnosis

Mechanism through which Consciousness expresses a sense of personal doership in a body-mind organism; *see* doer, *maya*

doer, doership

For the impersonal functioning of Consciousness, or God, through manifestation or life as we know it to happen, the basis of life is the sense of personal doership; Divine hypnosis creating the illusory ego's belief that it has free will; the sense of doership is unhappiness; spiritual seeking is the process of getting rid of personal doership; *see* ego, free will

dualism

The ego functions in dualism, which is the mental split between the "me" and the "other"; the mind, ego, does not accept the functioning of duality, the interdependence of opposites, but creates a conflict between the two members of a pair of opposites by wanting one in exclusion of the other (good-bad, beautiful-ugly, easy-difficult); what is absent in enlightenment is dualism; *see* duality

duality

Pairs of interconnected opposites, neither of which can exist without the other (i.e., happy-unhappy, positive-negative, light-dark); one of the essential mechanisms by which the totality of manifestation functions; when the ego becomes involved, duality becomes dualism; *see* ego, dualism, functioning

dvaita

Two, dual; *see* Advaita

education

Accumulation of concepts; to one degree or another a necessity for living in society; "learned ignorance"; *see* concept

ego

The sense of personal doership; Consciousness-in-action assuming identification as a "doer," thinking mind, with a separate name and form; the user of the word ego must know that the primary meaning is the mistaken belief of being a "doer," because a sage continues to have name and form, a body-mind organism, but *without* a sense of being a "doer"; *see* Consciousness-in-action, body-mind organism, Divine hypnosis, thinking mind

enlightenment

The spontaneous impersonal event at the end of the process of seeking in which there is the spontaneous, intuited, total understanding in the heart that there is no doer and never was a doer or seeker—the ego, the "me," is completely annihilated; *see* doer, ego, seeker, seeking

free will

All there is is Consciousness, there is absolutely no free will; everything is God's will, the impersonal functioning of Consciousness, manifesting as destiny, individual or otherwise; decisions have to be made, so one makes them *as if* there is free will—the result is God's

will; *see* destiny
functioning

Consciousness is all there is. There is no doer, no seeker, no decision maker, no lover, *but* there is *doing, seeking, deciding, loving*; functioning is the impersonal movement of Consciousness-in-action that gives the manifestation the *appearance of being real*. For example, the ego, sense of personal doership, interprets as "its functioning" that which is always and can only be the impersonal "functioning" of Consciousness through a body-mind organism; *see* manifestation

Gayatri

A verse from the Vedas used as a mantra

God

Consciousness, Source; not an entity; not personal; *see* Consciousness

grace

The totality of manifestation is grace; the prevalent misunderstanding is the ego's involvement in dualism and thus not accepting What-Is as grace; the ego refers to what is difficult as God's will and what is special and beneficial as God's grace; *see* dualism, involvement, What-Is

gunas

Attributes, qualities; the three primary attributes of the totality of manifestation are *sattva*, *rajas*, and *tamas*; *see* each attribute

Guru

Spiritual preceptor; the living expression of the Sadguru that has no sense of personal doership and through which a seeker may experience his or her True Nature; *see* Sadguru

Guru Purnima

The full moon (*purnima*) day in July-August on which the disciple renews his or her dedication to the Guru

happens, happening

This indicates an occurrence without any doer doing anything; the impersonal functioning of Consciousness-in-action; "happens" is spontaneous and without intention or volition, although there usually appears to be a chain of events, cause and effect, which leads to something that *just happens*. The meaning of this word is best conveyed by two examples:

- "The teaching *happens* through Ramesh." In other words, there is no "one" who does anything. It, the teaching, *happens*.

- "There is no seeker. The seeking is just *happening*."

heart

The understanding becomes complete when it is spontaneously intuited in the heart; in the heart there is intuited understanding, there is no "me" to understand anything; *see* intellect

horizontal

The involvement of the thinking mind; *see* involvement, thinking

Mind

I Am

The initial manifestation of impersonal Consciousness in the awareness I Am, other than which nothing exists; the only Truth since It cannot be disputed—thus It is not a concept unless conceived by subsequent thinking based on the feeling of a personal identity; the interval between two thoughts, between two expectations; *see* Consciousness, I-I

I-I

Ramana Maharshi's reference to Consciousness, Source, Totality; I-I and I Am are not two, I-I becomes I Am in manifestation, I-I becomes aware of Itself as I Am; *see* Consciousness, I Am

intellect

The understanding usually begins in the thinking mind—for the understanding to be complete and final it must be intuited in the heart; a well developed and concentrated intellect is necessary for the process of seeking on the path of jnana and dealing competently with the manifestation; *see* heart, thinking mind

involvement

The nonacceptance of What-Is; the cause of suffering; the ego's mistaken belief that it has free will and consequently in a continuous state of being judgmental, deciding, and being concerned about consequences; this concept correlates to the concept of attachment in Buddhism; *see* ego, free will, thinking mind, What-Is

Ishwara

In Hinduism Consciousness-in-action deified as in charge of the Universe

Janaka

King Janaka is the "superbly ripe disciple" of his Guru, Ashtavakra, in the *Ashtavakra Gita* translated by Ramesh in his book *A Duet of One*

japa

"muttering"; constant, it repels all other thoughts; vocal,

it becomes mental and is the same as meditation
jiva
    The individual, identified consciousness; *see* ego
jnana
    Understanding, especially the total, spontaneous, intuited understanding in the heart; understanding and acceptance as a path to enlightenment; jnana and bhakti are not two, however, bhakti becomes jnana prior to enlightenment (even if it is a split second before); *see* bhakti, jnani
Jnaneshwar
    A great Indian sage who was fundamentally a jnani, but from the *abhangas* he wrote it can be seen that he symbolises within himself a unity not only of jnana and bhakti but also yoga in its various aspects; the *Jnaneshwar* classic *Anubhavamrita*, or *Amritanubhava*, is translated by Ramesh in his book *Experience of Immortality*
jnani
    One who understands; currently used to refer to a seeker following the path of jnana as distinguished from that of bhakti, however, jnana and bhakti are not two; *see* bhakti, jnana, seeker
karma
    Consciousness manifesting as action which is the principle of cause and effect; one of the fundamental, functioning mechanisms of the totality of manifestation for life to happen as we know it; a cause, action, leads to an effect which in turn becomes a cause leading to another effect, and so on; *see* functioning, manifestation
kriya
    Spontaneous   movement(s)   or   reaction(s)   of

the body-mind organism caused by movement of the *kundalini* energy

kundalini

In Hinduism, an aspect of the feminine creative energy symbolised as a serpent lying dormant at the base of the spine until aroused; a potentially dangerous practice; the arising of the *kundalini* is not a prerequisite for enlightenment; *see* enlightenment

liberation

see enlightenment

lila

In Hinduism the play or game of God; the totality of manifestation looked upon as the Divine play; *see* destiny, manifestation

maha

Great; usually a prefix to a noun making it great or superior

Maheshwara

see Shiva

manifestation

Consciousness unmanifest reflected within Itself as the totality of What-Is; *see* Consciousness, *maya*

mantra

Instrument of thought; hymn, incantation; ideal or sacred sounds of certain syllables or words, the repetition of which may lead to material or spiritual benefits—if it is the destiny of the body-mind organism repeating them

maya

Illusion; delusion; the veiling power which conceals Consciousness unmanifest from Consciousness *reflected* within Itself as the totality of manifestation;

the identification with the body-mind organism as a separate individual and doer; *see* Consciousness, doer, manifestation

"me"

    see ego

meditation

    When meditation happens you know it because there is a feeling of emptiness; some body-mind organisms are not programmed to meditate so there is no question of right or wrong about meditating; not a must but if it happens it is good; involves a doer if there is effort and expectation; for the beginner, meditate on the fact that "you" have no free will; that meditation is true meditation in which there is no doer of the meditation; *see* doer, free will, sadhana

mind

    Consciousness-in-action as a functioning of thoughts received and subsequent thinking (the *physical mechanism* for receiving and spontaneously reacting to thought is the brain); the processing of thoughts received takes place in either of the two aspects of mind—working mind or thinking mind—in the latter the ego is involved; the destruction of the thinking mind, which can only be God's will, is the intuited understanding in the heart that there is no doer, no separation from Consciousness, which is the *essence* of mind; *see* brain, thinking mind, thought, working mind

moksha

    Liberation; *see* enlightenment

nirguna

    Without form or attributes

Nisargadatta Maharaj

Ramesh's final Guru; his teachings can be found in Ramesh's book *Pointers from Nisargadatta Maharaj*

Noumenon

Consciousness unmanifest; there is no plural for this word; *see* Consciousness

Now

see What-Is

observing

In observing there is an observer, an ego; *see* ego, witnessing

Om

see **Aum**

play

see lila

pool of Consciousness

A concept referring to energies which may or may not have been manifested as matter or non-matter in general or specifically as a body-mind organism; at the dissolution of matter or the death of a body-mind organism the energies return to the pool of Consciousness and may or may not again appear manifested; *see* rebirth

pradakshina

Devotional circumambulation of a sacred object or holy place

Prajna

Unselfconscious Knowledge; *see* Consciousness

predestination

see destiny

Present Moment

see What-Is

programming

Genes plus conditioning, over which the body mind organism has no control, determines the way the brain reacts to all input; the mechanism by which the destiny of a body-mind organism is carried out; *see* body-mind organism, brain, conditioning, destiny, ego

psychosomatic apparatus

see body-mind organism

puja

Ceremonial or ritual worship

rajas

Motivity, activity, energy; one of the three *gunas*; refers to the activating aspect of manifestation without which the other constituents could not manifest their inherent qualities; *see gunas*

Ramakrishna

The great Bengali bhakta sage who lived at Dakshineshwar in Calcutta in the nineteenth century

Ramana Maharshi

The great jnani sage of Arunachala who lived all of his adult life in Tiruvannamalai, Tamil Nadu; Ramesh said in satsang, "To me, in phenomenality, there is nothing higher than Ramana Maharshi."

realisation

see enlightenment

rebirth

There is no individual so there can be no rebirth of that which does not exist; there are past births and from them, at the deaths of the body-mind organisms, the functioning energies return to the pool of Consciousness to perhaps again, in another combination, pass into a future body mind organism—thus there are apparent past-life memories by some body-mind organisms of prior births; eventually, energies of such refinement may come together in a body-mind organism in which the process of seeking ends in enlightenment; *see* enlightenment, body-mind organism, ego, pool of Consciousness

rishi

Ancient sage

Sadguru

The Guru within you—the Self, or Consciousness

sadhaka

A seeker who practices sadhana; *see* sadhana

sadhana

Spiritual practice or practices involving a doer (seeker) which may precede the goal of enlightenment; the goal *may* or may not happen depending upon the destiny of the seeker; if sadhana happens, let it happen; traditional sadhanas are meditation, yoga, and selfless service (*seva*); a body-mind organism may be programmed to do one type of sadhana and not another; Ramesh's only recommended sadhana is analysis or investigation of actions

sage

A body-mind organism in which enlightenment has happened; a sage may be regarded as saintly, but a saint is not necessarily a sage; *see* enlightenment

saguna

With form and attributes

saint

see sage

samadhi

A state of meditation beyond mind; absorption in the Self

Sat

Existence, Being; *see Sat-Chit-Ananda*

Sat-Chit-Ananda

Being-Consciousness-Peace; in Hinduism the three "attributes" of attributeless Brahman, or the Source; *see* Consciousness

satsang

Association with the Truth—or one who has the Understanding

sattva

Being, existence, reality; one of the three *gunas*; it stands for equilibrium and manifests itself as light; *see gunas*

seeker

The ego mistakenly believing it is a doer and separate and thus a seeker seeking something sought; *see* ego, seeking

seeking

One of the innumerable and *impersonal* processes of Consciousness manifest; "from the first moment a baby seeks its mother's breast intuitively, life is nothing but seeking," regardless of what it is for; that there is no doer and no thing done and thus no seeker and no thing sought is the final understanding prior to the end of the process of seeking; *see* enlightenment, ego

Self-realisation

see enlightenment

seva

Selfless service, service without any expectations
shakti

Power, energy, capacity; in the totality of manifestation of Consciousness, or Shiva, within Itself, *shakti* is portrayed as the female energy of duality, Shiva-Shakti; she is deified, often with the name of Parvati, as the wife of Shiva; *see* Shiva
Shankara

Also called Adi Shankara and Shankaracharya; an eighth century philosopher and reformer of Hinduism who established the school of unqualified Advaita Vedanta
Shiva

Consciousness unmanifest; when manifest he is portrayed as the male energy of duality, Shiva-Shakti; he is deified as the husband of Shakti; one of the gods of the Hindu trinity; *see shakti*, trinity
siddha

Refers to a perfected sage (but with the understanding that *siddhis* are not necessary or prerequisite to enlightenment); often used to refer to one who has psychic powers or "gifts"
siddhi

The final "accomplishment" or enlightenment; has come to mean psychic power (which is often an obstruction to enlightenment because the ego becomes involved)
silence

Noninvolvement or nonidentification with thought(s); a sage is always in silence; silence between the Guru and the disciple is heart-to-heart speech; *see* involvement, sage

Source

> *see* Consciousness

split mind

> *see* whole mind

tamas

> Darkness, inertia, passivity, restraint; one of the three *gunas*; *see gunas*

Tao

> *see* Consciousness

thinking

> The functioning of thoughts received by the brain which can either be uninvolved as in the working mind or involved as in the thinking mind; *see* brain, functioning, thinking mind, thought, working mind

thinking mind

> The horizontal aspect of mind in which the ego is involved with thinking and concerned with *future consequences* for itself—i.e., worry or anxiety for whether an action will be beneficial or harmful, or for what others may think; not accepting What-Is; both the thinking mind and the working mind judge, but the thinking mind is also judgmental; both the thinking mind and the working mind are involved in what is being done, but the thinking mind thinks "'I' am doing it" and is personally concerned with future consequences; *see* horizontal, thought, What-Is, working mind

thought

> Thought does not originate in the body-mind organism, it comes from outside and a split-second later the brain spontaneously reacts according to its

programming; a thought is an input which brings about an output which leads to causation; both thought and the reaction(s) of the brain are vertical, in the Present Moment—if the ego gets involved (the thinking mind) then there is horizontal involvement in time; *see* brain, Present Moment, programming, thinking mind, working mind

Tiruvannamalai

The town in the state of Tamil Nadu in south-east India where Ramana Maharshi spent his entire adult life at the foot of the holy hill Arunachala

Totality

see Consciousness

trinity

The Hindu trinity is Brahma the creator, Vishnu the preserver, and Shiva—or Maheshwara—the destroyer

Tukaram

One of India's greatest bhakta sages who, following enlightenment, wrote devotionally as a pure jnani; wrote *abhangas* which have been set to music and are sung as **bhajans**

understanding, total

The spontaneous, intuited understanding in the heart that there is no doer; *see* enlightenment, doer

Unicity

see Consciousness

Upanishads

Concerned with pure knowledge, these ancient philosophical texts are much later than the original Vedas; the texts from which all Vedanta philosophy originates; *see* Vedanta, Vedas

Vedanta

Literally, the end of the Vedas, the culmination of knowledge; philosophy based upon the Upanishads; Advaita Vedanta is the most well-known branch of Vedanta; *see* dvaita, Upanishads

Vedas

The most ancient of the sacred literature of Hinduism; they start out as mythical and ritual texts and culminate in the pure philosophy of Vedanta; *see* Vedanta

vertical

Being in the Present Moment, or What-Is; cuts off horizontal involvement; only the working mind is functioning; *see* horizontal, What-Is, working mind

Vishnu

One of the gods of the Hindu trinity; *see* trinity

What-Is

Outside of space-time It neither is nor is not—past, present, and future and all of their apparent contents are *spontaneously* happening *simultaneously*; this state/non-state is also referred to as Present Moment and Here and Now; cannot be "experienced" by the ego

whole mind

Consciousness-in-action, I Am, is whole mind and becomes split or divided when identified with the body-mind organism as a "me"; (Note: whole mind/split mind and working mind/thinking mind are two different concepts and cannot be compared or interchanged); *see* split mind

witnessing

In witnessing there is no "one" doing the

witnessing, there is no ego present; see ego, observing
working mind

The vertical aspect of mind which is only in the Present Moment—the ego is not present with its concerns for future consequences; the working mind uses judgement and consideration of consequence to do the best it can with the knowledge it has for a task, but the judging and consideration of consequence are *in the Present Moment*, or What-Is, and there is *no* personal concern for *future* consequences; while the working mind is functioning there is little or no sense of time and place unless such consideration is part of the task at hand; in the sage there is *only* the working mind, there is *no* thinking mind; (Note: working mind/thinking mind and whole mind/split mind are two different concepts and cannot be compared or interchanged); see thinking mind, vertical, What-Is

∼